Circle of Faith

Enjoy!

Sally Dagnall

Published by Vineyard Stories
RR 1, Box 65-B9, Edgartown, MA 02539
508 221 2338
www.vineyardstories.com

Library of Congress Number: 2010925544

ISBN 9780977138494

Editor: Jan Pogue, Vineyard Stories
Designer: Sue Dawson

Photos courtesy the Abby Armstrong/Tuckernuck Antiques collection pages 28, 53, 88
Photos courtesy the Donald R. Andrew collection pages 50, 76, 100, 118
Photos courtesy of Chris Baer from the Stan Lair collection pages 116. 119, 128
Photo courtesy the Bogle collection page 23
Photos courtesy the Dagnall collection pages 40, 65, 72, 106, 136
Photos courtesy the Dagnall/Tucker collection pages 29, 77. 56, 96, 113, 124, 126
Photos courtesy the Harvey Garneau Jr. collection pages 14, 24, 37, 46, 47, 54, 62, 70, 73, 74, 75, 120, 122
Photo courtesy the Glass collection page 75
Photos courtesy the Sam Low collection pages 138, 139, 140, 141
Photos courtesy the Lowe collection pages 80, 81
Photos courtesy the Martha's Vineyard Museum collection pages 10, 13, 160
Photos courtesy Roy Meekins collection pages 44, 59, 67, 78, 121, 143
Photos courtesy the MVCMA collection pages 19, 20, 22, 26, 32, 36, 38, 52, 60, 84, 86, 91, 93, 95, 97, 98, 99, 103, 110, 112
Photos courtesy the Estelle Reagan collection page 135
Photos courtesy the Stannard/Riedinger collection pages 30, 34, 66, 68, 69, 87, 130, 133
Photos courtesy the W. Douglas Thompson collection pages 61, 82, 90, 92, 99, 101, 111, 126, 127
Photos courtesy the Doug Ulwick collection pages 27, 43, 48, 58, 64, 79, 94, 96, 104, 107, 108, 125, 142
Front cover: MVCMA collection
Back cover: Martha's Vineyard Museum collection

Printed in Canada

Circle of Faith

The Story of the Martha's Vineyard Camp-Meeting

By Sally Dagnall

Errata

p. 11 Should read "The twenty four states..."

p 37 "School Street" labelled on the drawing should be "Vineyard Avenue".

p.106 Caption should read; "The present day carbon fiber cross erected in 2008"

Dedication

In honor of all campgrounders, past and present,
who made and continue to make and preserve this
wonderful place; and to my grandparents and
parents who brought me here.

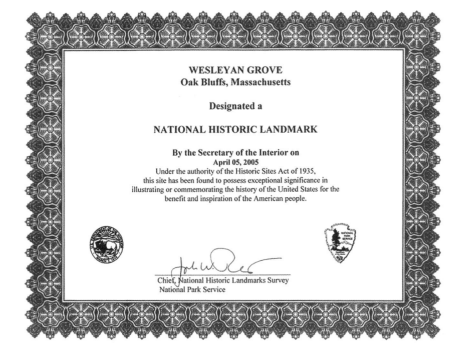

WESLEYAN GROVE
Oak Bluffs, Massachusetts

Designated a

NATIONAL HISTORIC LANDMARK

By the Secretary of the Interior on
April 05, 2005
Under the authority of the Historic Sites Act of 1935,
this site has been found to possess exceptional significance in
illustrating or commemorating the history of the United States for the
benefit and inspiration of the American people.

Chief, National Historic Landmarks Survey
National Park Service

Contents

Introduction

Tradition and Timelessness

Walking the streets of the Martha's Vineyard Camp-Meeting Association, a community of charming painted cottages with a central wrought-iron tabernacle, is like entering another world and another time. Established 175 years ago as a religious summer retreat, the thirty-four-acre parcel of land, with grounds arranged in concentric circles and parks around the central Trinity Park, draws thousands of visitors each year. It was the model for many post–Civil War religious camp-meeting sites around the country and has been the subject of novels, histories, and photo books.

Although directly responsible for the development of the lively beach town of Oak Bluffs and only a few yards from a busy commercial district, it is as different from its progeny as any parent could be: It is a place of peace and tranquility, its colorful cottages huddled together on small lots heavily planted with oaks and other foliage, its way of life one of old-fashioned courtesy, deep family connections, and rules that stemmed from the stern admonitions of Methodist preachers.

Strangely, the establishment of the Methodist camp-meeting grounds in 1835 as a permanent fixture on the Island seven miles off the coast of Massachusetts was something of an accident of time and place. That accident, however, has had a significant impact on many worlds — architecture, religion, the Island of

Martha's Vineyard itself, and generations of people who found rest and respite as they returned year after year. The resulting community, while no longer dedicated to any one religious denomination, reflects the lives of the people who once wandered the grounds in the past and those who live there today.

The campgrounds were declared a National Historic Landmark in 2005, which recognizes it as an important place in the history of the nation. The landmark status was built on many aspects, including the campgrounds' connection with the great religious camp-meeting movement of the early nineteenth century and the substantial recorded history of its first thirty-four years. The unusual layout of the grounds and the remarkable state of preservation of both the buildings and grounds, along with the recognized architectural form of the Martha's Vineyard Campgrounds cottage, make it a place unique in America.

That preservation and sense of the past is so strong that Pulitzer Prize–winning author/historian David McCullough once said, "If an Association member from 1875 traveled forward in time … and toured the campgrounds, he or she would feel quite at home."

The 314 cottages, five Association buildings, and other properties on the grounds are a direct link to the Vineyard's past. To read the story of how this came about is to understand what was once described as a chance to peek inside the "charmed circle around the preaching area (which) banished feelings of isolation and anxiety, the causes of greed and selfishness in city life."

It was a place, as this book shows you, where a group of people spent summers inside a circle of faith and which today continues as a place of tradition and timelessness.

Jeremiah Pease laid the lasting foundation for a religious movement which became the Martha's Vineyard Camp-Meeting Association. He served the camp-meeting in various capacities for twenty-two years.

Surely the Lord Is in This Place
1835

"This was the day of small beginnings."
HENRY BAYLIES

The year 1835 was a time of economic prosperity in the United States. The national debt had been paid off, and trade was increasing. The twenty-five states, with a population of almost thirteen million people, were bursting with activity and change. People were looking for new frontiers, many heading west on the Oregon Trail, traveling into territories that were wild and unsettled. In the states themselves, many things were changing: the industrial revolution, slavery, prohibition.

At the same time, people seemed to be seeking answers beyond daily life, and it was a period of great religious revival in the United States, a movement called the Second Great Awakening. The Awakening was typified in the early 1800s by a religious camp-meeting movement led by Presbyterians, Baptists, and Methodists. The evangelistic movement started in Kentucky with revival-like meetings attended by thousands. It swept throughout the country and fostered change in prison reform, abolitionism, and temperance. Although the Presbyterians and the Baptists soon lost their enthusiasm for the movement, Methodists continued to embrace camp-meetings with fervor.

None of this meant much to Jeremiah Pease, who lived in Edgartown with his wife and ten children. Pease, like most residents of Martha's Vineyard, was isolated from mainland America and little affected by events there. Life on the Vineyard was simple, hard, and little changed from generation to generation. The people were industrious, independent, and proud. They made their living from the water, and they raised their food with their own hard toil.

Pease, who was born in 1792, was a typical Islander. He held many jobs — a surveyor, a lighthouse keeper, a shoemaker, politician, salesman of molasses and whale oil, and a justice of the peace.

The Island was a major whaling center, and as many as six hundred of the Island's almost three thousand inhabitants were living at sea on whaling vessels at any one time. Pease himself owned shares in whaling vessels. Much of the rest of the population worked at the trades connected with whaling: Shipwrights built the wooden boats that carried the men to sea; chandlers provided supplies and equipment for the ships; local craftsmen made sails and casks to hold the rich whale oil; bakeries spent much of their time cooking hardtack for the long whaling voyages.

Farmers, who were largely self-sufficient, occasionally supplemented their needs by trading Island goods with passing vessels. They raised vegetables and livestock and looked to the ponds and surrounding waters for sources of food. A boat was considered an essential part of a farmer's equipment.

Despite the Island's isolation, religion had always been a part of the Vineyard. The members of the local Wampanoag Tribe were deeply religious, believing in two great spirits — one the maker of mankind, and the other the ruler of evil. Some in the tribe were converted to Christianity by Thomas Mayhew Jr., who ministered to them and to his small flock of white settlers in the mid-1600s. As the years passed, the Congregational Church emerged as the primary denomination on the Island, particularly in the larger settlement of Edgartown.

Yet the religious climate on the Vineyard in the early 1800s, just as on the mainland, was ripe for change. The Congregational Church in Edgartown was being split apart over a theological dispute between Unitarianism and Trinitarianism. Many wealthier and more educated members of the congregation, led by the long-tenured and politically active Rev. Joseph Thaxter, were leaning toward Unitarianism, which left others, like Pease, feeling left out.

Although it had little presence at that time on the Vineyard, Methodism provided comfort and was considered a religion for the common man. It had begun in England in 1729 with John Wesley and came to the U.S. in the 1760s. Methodism reached out to the poor, encouraged its followers to help one another, and was concerned with the social inequities of the time. The religion preached that personal salvation could be reached through good works, avoiding evil deeds, and living by the edicts of God. The tenets of the church made the independent and self-sufficient Vineyarders feel they could control their own lives and salvation through their own efforts and good works rather than through dictates from established churches.

This new religion first appeared on the Vineyard in 1787 with the arrival of John Saunders and his wife, who had been slaves in Virginia. Saunders occasionally spoke to groups of people of color, and on the Vineyard he addressed small enclaves of African Americans who lived here. Yet the religion was slow to take hold; in 1809, when Methodist evangelist Rev. Erastus Otis arrived on the Vineyard, there were only nine members of the faith. He brought a new style of preaching that appealed to many but was disdained by traditionalists. Because of the schism on the Island, the Methodist adherents kept their beliefs private, and meetings were often held in out-of-the way places and in private homes.

Yet the stealth needed to practice the religion did not seem to impede the growth of Methodism, and by 1821 there were three groups meeting, one in each of the villages of Edgartown, Holmes Hole (now Vineyard Haven), and West Tisbury.

By then, the Island had grown more welcoming of Methodists, and had begun to attract itinerant preachers like Rev. John "Reformation John" Adams, who had converted to Methodism as a

The man who kept the records

Martha's Vineyard Museum Collection

Hebron Vincent was a self-educated minister, attorney, historian, and one of the founding fathers of the MVCMA. He served as camp-meeting secretary for thirty-four years.

EARLY CAMP-MEETINGS were held in different places at unscheduled times. As a result, there are few records of those meetings. This camp-meeting was the first to establish permanency, to form a group to organize those meetings, and to maintain records of them. Hebron Vincent was appointed its first secretary in 1835, serving in that capacity on and off until 1869. He kept personal records of those meetings and ultimately wrote two detailed volumes, published in 1858 and 1869, about the meetings held in Wesleyan Grove. These books constitute the only substantial contemporary chronicle of any American camp-meeting.

Hebron Vincent was a self-educated teacher of many talents serving as an attorney, a registrar of probate for Dukes County, and a Methodist minister. He was a community leader who was as fervent an abolitionist as he was Methodist. He was a distant younger cousin, on his mother's side, of Jeremiah Pease, and they maintained a close relationship, including the nine-year apprenticeship he served under Pease learning the trade of cordwaining (shoemaker).

Vincent insisted that he was writing about a place as well as an event and an institution. This sense of place, one "hallowed by a thousand Christian associations," forever reverberating with ancient gospel sermons, earnest prayers, "pathetic appeals to the unconverted, and exhilarating songs of praise," never leaves his prose.

Campground attendees gathered for worship in Wesleyan Grove. Children, originally not part of camp-meetings, had begun to attend by the time this photo was taken.

young man and traveled throughout New England. When Jeremiah Pease heard Adams preach on the Vineyard in May 1822 for the funeral of a friend, he was deeply moved. He later attended a joint Methodist/Baptist revival meeting on the Vineyard; within four months of hearing Adams' fiery preaching, Pease converted to Methodism.

Jeremiah Pease took his new religion very seriously, although his own wife and children (except for his son, Jeremiah Jr.) seem not to have embraced it as he did. By 1833 he had become a licensed exhorter — a Methodist title for a lay person who urges and admonishes earnestly — and had begun to conduct services as a layman. During this time religious fervor was sweeping the Island, and for many Islanders religion became the most important activity aside from daily chores. Pease, closely attuned to the religious climate on the Vineyard, began to believe it would benefit Islanders to have a simple retreat where they could gather together to praise God and get away from the problems of everyday life.

Pease, along with six Edgartown friends who were also staunch Methodists, began to make plans for a camp-meeting, choosing a site Jeremiah may have discovered while traveling from Edgartown to the small settlement of Eastville, just outside the current Vineyard Haven, where he served as a lay preacher to a small congregation.

The Edgartown men were all well respected on Martha's Vineyard. Thomas W. Coffin was a master mariner whose family arrived on the Vineyard in 1682. Chase Pease came from another branch of Jeremiah's own family. Frederick Baylies was the last missionary to the Martha's Vineyard Wampanoag

Indians employed by the Society for Propagating the Gospel. Besides serving as a missionary and preacher, Baylies designed three of Edgartown's early churches, including the Federated Church and the Old Whaling Church. Three other Methodist leaders, Hebron Vincent, Daniel Webb, who was the presiding elder of the Methodist District, and James C. Bontecou, pastor of the Methodist church in Edgartown, joined him in planning the first camp-meeting. Hebron Vincent would later become the official recorder of campground news for thirty-four years.

The site Pease chose was isolated and difficult to reach. It was located in a grove of oaks on a sheep pasture owned by Farm Neck farmer William Butler about seven miles outside the center of Edgartown and six miles from Holmes Hole. The area was named Quasquannes and was called "the place of the big trees" by the Wampanoag.

The few roads that went between the two villages where the land lay were little more than rough cart-paths. It was easier to get to the spot by water, bringing food, bedding, and clothing, landing at Norris Wharf at the small settlement of Eastville, then hiking just over a mile on sandy tracks that ran along fenced pasturage, down the hill on what is now Vineyard Avenue, and across the swamp head of Squash Meadow Pond (now Lake Anthony and Sunset Lake).

Three of the original organizers agreed to pay Butler $15 to use the land and promised to rectify any damage to the woods, fences, or sheep.

The week before the camp-meeting, Thomas Coffin and his sons, Sirson P. and John Wesley, and Frederick Baylies and his son, Henry, came to prepare the site. Henry later described the long trip from Edgartown Harbor to the meeting place by recalling, "A vessel was freighted at Edgartown with lumber, sails, etc. for the new camping-ground. Her cargo was rafted ashore on the east side of the (East) Chop. It was a hard day's work to get the material ashore and up to the grove, but it was done and the preachers' stand was partially constructed that same day."

They cleared the underbrush, placed two barrels close to the edge of Squash Meadow Pond for a supply of pure water, and erected a small rough shed called the preachers' tent to serve as the quarters for the ministers. It contained an elevated seat and stand to be used as a pulpit. There were plenty of bundles of rye-straw upon the bare ground for the campers to spread for bedding, luxurious accommodations for the clergy since one observer stated, "Fortunate, indeed, was the man of the cloth who had a quilt to cover him and an extra sheaf of straw for a pillow."

An interpretation of the preachers' stand and society/church tents under the "venerable oaks" in Wesleyan Grove.

On the ground in front of the preachers' tent was a twenty-five-by-twelve-foot railed enclosure that served as a temporary altar with seats for the singers during public worship or for penitent sinners following public prayer meetings. In front of the altar were backless rough board seats for the congregation. Large lanterns hung on two stately oaks located on either side of the preachers' stand to illuminate the ministers during evening services. The whole encampment at that time did not cover more than half an acre.

Conditions were primitive, and attendees had to transport everything they needed for the six days of the camp-meeting. Henry Baylies wrote that during that first camp-meeting, "Owing to a storm and the non-arrival of a vessel which was to bring us supplies, we got short of provisions, and John W. (John Wesley Coffin) and myself were started out on a foraging expedition. We succeeded and at noon time brought in from a farm house nearby a large tin pail full of salt junk, potatoes, turnips, parsnips, etc. which were spread for our dinner."

Nine church society tents reflecting the membership in attendance were arranged in a semi-circle at the rear of the site behind the benches for the worshipers. The tents were built of rough joists and covered with superannuated sails (sails too old to be used on ships) of various patterns. Canvas was propped in front of each for an awning under which meals could be taken. The tents were furnished with chests and trunks and a bench or two. Canvas was hung down the middle to separate the sleeping quarters of the men and women, all of whom slept on the ground.

The landings

WHEN THOMAS COFFIN AND FREDERICK BAYLIES, along with their sons, arrived to set up the original site, they probably landed on the beach in the area of the present-day Oak Bluffs Wharf (#1 on map). Later, there were four principal landings.

Norris's Wharf at Eastville (#2), located approximately one mile from the site, was the first used by people coming from Holmes Hole (now Vineyard Haven) and from the Cape. After landing there, people then hiked about a mile to the grounds.

In 1866, a dock was built in Eastville at the foot of what is now New York Avenue (#3), which shortened the trip to the campgrounds considerably. The Oak Bluffs Land and Wharf Company built its wharf on the site of the present Oak Bluffs Wharf in 1867 (#4).

This remained the preferred landing because of its location until the Vineyard Grove Company built its wharf in 1872, approximately where the East Chop Beach Club is located, and it was adopted by the MVCMA as its official landing (#5).

Drawing by Doug Ulwick

The first camp-meeting began on August 24 with the Rev. Thomas C. Pierce, a Methodist clergyman, conducting the first public exercise Monday evening. The camp-meeting was very serious in nature, with no children in attendance and a set of rules and regulations read daily from the stand. Religious services were held morning, afternoon, and evening, with additional prayer meetings in the tents and hymn singing at all hours. The six-day meeting was one of great spirituality, and Hebron Vincent, who had been appointed secretary, noted later, "The preaching was in the demonstration of the spirit and of power; usually followed by warm and forcible applications and exhortations, inspiring those in attendance that, surely the Lord is in this place."

Although later camp-meetings would attract thousands from many places, attendees of this first camp-meeting were primarily from the Vineyard and the neighboring mainland. There is no record of how many attended the first meeting, but Hebron Vincent reported that sixty-five people were converted, including "men of high respectability." At the last morning service, two or three hundred "testified that God had deepened the work of grace in their hearts during the meeting. Six more souls were reclaimed at that time."

An artist's rendition of the early camp-meeting with grove of trees, crude preachers' stand, worshipers, and society tents in the background. Although it was isolated and a difficult spot to reach, the camp-meeting early on attracted thousands.

A licensed boarding tent on the grounds with signs admonishing diners to have tickets before taking a seat. Bracketed oil lamps with mercury glass reflectors are mounted to the post in the foreground to provide nighttime illumination.

Departure and Return to the "Leafy Sanctuary"

1836~1849

"This sacred retreat ... seemed to us more glorious than ever before."

HEBRON VINCENT

Although camp-meetings were generally held only once in any given location, the first meeting had been so successful that many of those who attended wanted to return the following year. The preachers voted to purchase, with money collected at the meeting, the lumber used to build the preachers' tent and seats after landowner William Butler gave permission to use the grove the following year.

This decision would have a dramatic influence on the character of the Vineyard as what had been temporary took one step toward permanency, and the Island's enforced isolation quietly and steadily began to be penetrated.

During the next several years, the camp-meeting under the oaks grew in size as word was spread by circuit riding preachers and traders. It began to at-tract people from Nantucket and all along the main-land coast who made their way to the Vineyard on a variety of sailing vessels. By 1837 there were twelve society tents (church tents), a small boarding tent or two, seventeen preachers, and 2,000 people within the encampment during the one-week Au-gust meeting. Three years later there were sixteen society tents with some new smaller auxiliary tents established by occupants who desired both space and privacy.

The spot itself continued to be heralded for its beauty and tranquility, and the camp-meeting was praised for its organization and convenience. Rev. Franklin Fisk, writing about the 1838 meeting, noted, "I have attended three camp meetings on this ground, and have heard many ministers express their opinion in regard to its location and other conveniences … that in any respect it is not excelled by any spot which they have ever seen, and that in all respects, considered collectively it excels them all. I know not how it could be much improved."

People continued to bring everything they needed for the week. The lack of refrigeration made it a challenge for the women to keep the food in good condition during the warm August weather. Most of the food was prepared at home, although some cooking was done over open fires. Tables were set up behind the circle of tents where meals were served under the shade of the trees.

Martha's Vineyard was not the only camp-meeting in the state; the meetings had become significant enough that the State Legislature passed the Act For the Protection of Camp-Meetings Against Disturbance on April 17, 1838. At the same time, the Vineyard camp was unusual because of its longevity; most camps stayed a year or two in one place, then moved on.

In 1840, spurred by that longevity, the name "Wesleyan Grove" was formally adopted for the Vineyard camp-meeting, and camp leaders took a five-year lease that included the grove of oaks plus a large section of adjacent lands known as the "Great Pasture." That year, too, the camp's ministers authorized the purchase of a book for the secretary to record the happenings of the camp-meetings. Prior to this, the secretary's annual report had been published in the *Zion's Herald*, the official Methodist journal. This seemingly small step began to create a record that 170 years later would allow researchers to trace the camp's history in an almost unprecedented fashion.

The next nine years were a time of growth and increasing popularity. In 1841 there were twenty large society tents in the front circle and several family tents housing nearly 800 people; by 1844 the number of tents had grown to more than forty, housing over 1,100 people. Ten feet were added to the west end of the preachers' tent to accommodate the increasing number of ministers serving the camp.

That same year, the meeting secretary, Brother George F. Pool, predicted the Vineyard camp-meeting was "destined to rise in importance and the Wesleyan Grove in future years may become a rallying point for multitudes. A convenient landing, level ground, a delightful grove, and an abundant supply of the sweetest water, are among the inducements which this place holds out to the lovers of camp-meetings."

MVCMA collection

The Power Street Methodist Church society tent and congregation from Providence, Rhode Island.

Protecting the righteous

Bogle collection

IN 1838, the state of Massachusetts passed a law to give direct protection to the camp-meetings. The law, in part, reads:

Any person who, during the time of holding any camp or field meetings for religious purposes, shall, within one mile of the place of holding such meeting, hawk or peddle any goods, wares, merchandise, or drinks, or practise [sic] or engage in any gaming or horse-racing, or exhibit, or offer to exhibit, any shows or plays, shall forfeit for each offence [sic] a sum not exceeding twenty dollars to be recovered on complaint made to any justice of the peace of the county in which the offence [sic] is committed: provided, however, that this act shall not be construed to require any person having his regular and usual place of business within the limits aforesaid to suspend such business.

A rigid sixteen-and-a-half-hour schedule was maintained during camp-meeting. The bell at the Tabernacle helped maintain order.

A view of Trinity Park showing a tent frame of one of the society tents that once lined the main circle around the preachers' stand. The parklike atmosphere of the campgrounds added greatly to its appeal.

Yet as the five-year lease obtained in November 1839 began to expire in 1844, those attending decided not to hold any more meetings in Wesleyan Grove. Hebron Vincent recorded that the decision was "not prompted by any want of appreciation of the excellence and advantages of the site, nor any feelings of hostility to the friends here." It was, he said, simply a decision that something new was needed. Vincent acknowledged that even he had some reservations. "It seemed almost sacrilegious to quit holding camp-meetings at this place."

Despite the conflicted feelings, all the fixtures including the preachers' stand, the benches, and every remnant of the more than forty tents was removed.

Although it was a sad parting, and many reluctantly left the spot hallowed by so many Christian victories and endearing associations, it was also a short one.

The camp-meeting of 1845 was held in Westport, Massachusetts. Although records show it had "good results," the location was difficult to reach by water and the land rough for camping. Many attendees missed the Vineyard and voted to return to the camp-meeting under the oaks. Another group organized a second camp-meeting in East Greenwich, Rhode Island.

A new lease was obtained for the Wesleyan Grove location from Steven H. and Harriet Bradley, who now owned the land, and the Methodists came home to a "leafy sanctuary" enlarged and furnished with new seats and a new preachers' stand more favorably located and comfortable. This had been accomplished by the efforts of Sirson P. Coffin, who would serve as agent of the grounds for more than twenty years. The cost for these preparations was $174.08, the first debt for the group and one that took three years to pay off.

The custom of holding preachers' prayer meetings, generally focusing on a specific topic, was adopted in 1846 and was perhaps the forerunner of Bible Study groups. The clergy took their calling seriously. Since one of their concerns was the conducting of business on Sundays, which they felt was a violation of God's laws, the elders in 1847 requested that the captains and owners of the steamboats not run their boats on the camp-meeting Sabbath. Since Sunday services at Wesleyan Grove began to attract thousands, that request quickly came to be ignored.

Once resettled on the Vineyard, the camp-meeting grew quickly. By 1848, there were sixty-four tents, and attendance at Sunday services was somewhere between two and three thousand. Over fifty ministers were in attendance in 1849, including a number of denominations other than Methodist. "Unquestionably, the great religious awakening which has pervaded the country the past year has been the procuring cause of the attendance of some thousands more at this time than would otherwise have presented themselves at our yearly 'feast of tabernacles,'" Vincent reported.

People came from all parts of New England and as far away as New York, Maryland, and Pennsylvania. Those who came from the mainland traveled on railroads to New Bedford and then on the steamers *Eagle's Wing* or *Island Home* or on smaller vessels from the south side of the Cape and elsewhere. Steamboats and sailing vessels came from Nantucket. Edgartown residents sailed from Edgartown, took wagons along Farm Neck Road as far as they could (about seven miles), and walked the rest of the way or ferried to Norris's Wharf at Eastville and hiked over the dunes or traveled by horseback.

The tent of the Hutchinson family, who were popular and well-known for their harmonic religious singing. They performed frequently at the camp-meetings.

Family tents, shown here with decorative scalloped edges that became the model for later filigree, provided home base for conversation, prayers, and congenial moments. Note the rusticate bench.

Those from Holmes Hole traveled by land (about seven and a half miles) around the Lagoon Pond or sailed to Norris's Wharf across the harbor.

Nothing seemed to stop them from coming. A cholera epidemic in the United States in 1849 seemed sure to impact attendance, and yet, as Vincent reported, the congregation was about the same as previous years. He maintained that people attending the camp-meeting in Wesleyan Grove had unusually good health due in part of the adoption of the regulations set by the Edgartown Board of Health, along with the care people took with their diet and the abundant supply of fresh water. But he was also convinced that just being at the camp-meeting and "drinking of the living fountain of salvation that gushes up so freely and plentifully here" was better than "a journey to the White Mountains, or a month's residence at Saratoga Springs."

The devoted attendees were living in a changing world where the rest and respite of the camp-meeting was a welcome break. It was the beginning of a decade of dramatic economic and cultural changes in the United States. The California Gold Rush began in 1848, and the Mexican-American War ended in 1849. Questions about slavery were beginning to split the country, while at the same time industrialization and advances in transportation and communication began to change mainland America.

Things were also beginning to change on the Vineyard. The *Vineyard Gazette*, started in 1846, became the Island's first newspaper, then offering more communication to a place starved for news of itself. The steamboat *Naushon* began sailing regularly between the Vineyard and the mainland, bringing an influx of visitors. The whaling industry of New England had its greatest single year, with the Vineyard serving as a port for many of the Nantucket whaling ships.

Attendance at the camp-meeting grew to such a number that changes in the layout of the grounds and more organization were required. To accomplish this, a Committee of Arrangements was authorized at the close of the 1847 camp-meeting to make plans for the following year's meeting, including adopting regulations on the prices of straw, milk cartage, and all other matters having reference to the financial interest of the meeting.

Abby Armstrong/Tuckernuck Antiques collection

Congregants from Bristol, Rhode Island, gather in front of their society tent. Tents represented dozens of communities up and down the East Coast.

The consecrated tree was a place where devoted men (and a few playful boys) from the campgrounds gathered for prayer and praise in 1849. Remains of this ancient tree may be seen today in Hartford Park between Pequot and Massasoit streets.

The wide canvas overhangs of the family tents provided cover from the elements and were suggestive of the deep roof overhangs of the present cottages.

Wesleyan Grove Takes Root
1850~1858

"Such another spot can hardly be found on earth so nearly resembling Eden in its primeval beauty and loveliness."

UNIDENTIFIED LOVER OF CAMP-MEETINGS

Worshiping at the camp-meetings was rigorous and demanding.

At the first streaks of daylight, the trumpet and later the bell sounded to announce the beginnings of the day's activities. Prayer meetings began at 6 a.m., breakfast was served at 7 a.m., and family and tent meetings were held from 8 a.m. to 10 a.m.

Over fifty preachers spoke to enthusiastic congregations daily in 1850 at 10 a.m., 2 p.m., and 7 p.m., and to a congregation of over 3,000 on the Sabbath. The ministers expected, and got, conversions and baptisms. Backsliders were reclaimed and souls quickened at these meetings. Shouts of "Hallelujah!" "Hosanna!" and "Praise the Lord!" were routine, and reports of "clean victories" and "all sanctified within the tents," were recorded by Hebron Vincent, the camp-meeting secretary. There was a seriousness of purpose that never wavered: The order of the meeting was never to be interrupted. There was no undue levity, no smile of contempt, no gatherings for fruitless discussions. "The Spirit of God prevailed in all hearts, and everyone who entered the sacred enclosure seemed to realize that it was holy ground," Vincent wrote.

In addition, public meetings, hymn sings, and gatherings of young people took place in the afternoons. At 10 p.m. all attendees returned to their tents for their final prayers before retiring.

Three ceremonies were an important part of the camp-meetings: the Sacrament of the Lord's Supper through communion, the Love Feast, and the Parting Ceremony.

Communion was received daily by both laity and ministers. The Love Feast took place on the last day of the meeting when all the campers assembled at the preachers' stand. Here, attendees testified about what they had experienced during the days of the camp-meeting or of other personal experiences.

The Parting Ceremony, which took place at the close of the meeting, was both impressive and emotional. Pairs joined hands and formed a circle while walking in procession within the circle of tents, singing hymns and then finally all halting. Facing their partners, they bid them a good-bye, each person then moving to the right, taking the next person by the hand and bidding them farewell until the full round had been made. Eventually, this ceremony was replaced by a more formal meeting at the preachers' stand because of the large number of participants.

But if the religious seriousness of the meetings hadn't changed, the atmosphere of the grounds had certainly changed since the return to the Vineyard in 1846, as evidenced by the festive air that now prevailed. Over the years, many of the devoted attendees had formed friendships, and friendly greetings opened each meeting. The social function of the gatherings was becoming as important as the religious.

The setting, too, had become an important part of the meeting. People realized they could both cleanse their souls and refresh their physical beings by taking advantage of the sea breezes and the healing and relaxing qualities of the ocean. By the 1857

MVCMA collection

Camp-meeting records show Thomas Kingsbury had a tent at 37 Washington Avenue (now Butler Avenue) from 1867 to 1869. He replaced it with a cottage in 1870 at the same location.

camp-meeting, people were arriving before the meeting and staying longer. While Vincent reported that the meetings had become more social and less spiritual in recent years, he still asserted, "A large portion of both the ministry and the laity was as devoted and laborious as ever, and oftentimes great numbers of sinners were saved."

Children began to come to the camp-meetings with their parents, and they attended prayer and church meetings. Special services were held at 1 p.m. daily for them in front of the preachers' stand. In 1848 a special children's baptism was held after the adult baptismal service. As the number of families attending the camp-meetings increased, the importance of early religious training was emphasized. As one church leader stated, "Within our children were the highest hopes of the church." For several years a minister from New Bedford regularly addressed the children on various subjects, on one occasion preaching strongly against the use of tobacco.

The camp-meetings lengthened from one week to ten days; and, while they were still primarily religious with public services three times a day followed by prayer meetings each afternoon, they also permitted participants to enjoy the beach and friends.

The campgrounds had become a community of

Nature and religion

WESLEYAN GROVE and the MVCMA were used as a model for many post–Civil War camp-meetings including Ocean Grove, New Jersey, and Bay View, Michigan.

When Bay View made its National Historic Landmark application, it referred to the Vineyard campgrounds, saying it "consciously united religion and recreation in a woodsy hideaway. The Vineyard camp meeting, with its hundreds of tiny cottages on little tent lots and a variety of communal parks, was often seen as a utopian social critique. Families in the 'charmed circle' around the preaching area banished feelings of isolation and anxiety, the causes of greed and selfishness in city life. Nature and experimental religion were the catalysts for a better, kinder society. All of this was uniquely American."

Rules adopted in 1853

THE RULES WERE POSTED and read daily from the stand.

1. The ground within the circle of the tents is sacredly set apart for religious services. There shall be no walking to and fro, or gathering together in companies for conversation of any kind, during public worship at the stand.
2. When the signal shall be given from the stand for preaching, all exercises in the tents must cease, and the people repair to the seats.
3. The hours for preaching shall be at 10 o'clock a.m., at 2 p.m., and at 7 in the evening.
4. There shall be a superintendent appointed by each tent's company, whose duty it shall be to preserve order in his tent, in accordance with the regulations of the meeting.
5. There shall be family devotions in each tent, morning and evening, with the reading of the Scriptures.
6. The hours for meals shall be, breakfast at 7 o'clock, dinner at 12, and tea at 5½.
7. There shall be no smoking of tobacco in the tents, nor within the circle of the tents.
8. There shall be a light kept burning in each tent all night.
9. The walks for retirement are, for the ladies, in the direction in the front of the stand, (being a south easterly direction there from, and including the space between the road leading from the ground to the east or nearest landing, and that leading to the point directly in the rear of the New Bedford Elm Street Tent,) and for gentlemen, in the direction in the rear of the stand.
10. The signal will be given each morning, at 5½ o'clock, for rising, and each tent-master is required to see that this rule is enforced in all the tents, large and small, under his supervision.
11. The signal will be given at 10 o'clock in the evening, at which time all vocal exercises must cease, and all persons not having lodgings on the ground must immediately retire from the same.

Members of the Morse family, residents of Edgartown, sit in front of their tent on Fisk Avenue. The families often erected small signs to announce ownership of their tents, as can be seen at the top of the tent.

tents. Larger society tents circled the preaching area, and smaller tents huddled close together behind them. Small boarding tents were located behind the last row of family tents. Rough wooden tables and benches were set up where the women prepared the food. The limited sanitary facilities were located away from the area in the open fields.

Families began to live in smaller family tents outside of the main circle. By 1855, of the 200 tents on the grounds, 150 were family tents.

Family tents ranged in cost from $50 to $400, and many were made by the women for their families. A story in the *Vineyard Gazette* in 1935 described the memories of Mrs. B. S. Kingman, who first came to the camp-meetings in 1870. She recalled her mother, Mrs. Barnabas Snow, making a tent cover on her sewing machine.

The ordinary family tent was floored and measured eight feet by twelve feet and consisted of a ridgepole with four upright poles for the corners and a covering. Larger tents occupied an area of twenty by forty-five feet with outhouses and had boards erected about six feet high on the sides with an outside flap of canvas stretched over a front porch.

At night in the smaller tents, curtains were used to separate sleeping compartments. In the daytime the bedding was tucked out of sight and furniture was brought out. The more elaborate tents were divided into the parlor and sleeping areas, and in some cases two tents were pitched together.

Many of these larger tents were extravagantly decorated and boasted of complete parlor and bedroom sets. A reporter from the *Boston Atlas and Bee* described "this display of men, women, and children in their own tents, which have been erected with much taste, furnished so neatly, and many of them with all the luxuries of a city drawing-room." Tents

and other items were often stored over the months between camp-meetings in wooden structures located behind the tents. Later, many of these structures would be joined to the future cottages.

While tents afforded comforts that could not otherwise be enjoyed, those same comforts also tended to keep a great many away from the preaching and prayer meetings. To avoid this, the camp-meeting leadership adopted rules requiring that members of each family tent had to be approved by a church. The name of the tent owner and the name of the church recommending him were posted on the tent, and each tent was under the supervision of the tent-master of the society or company approving it. Tents were also required to hang a lighted lantern at night and have a bucket of water ready at or near the front or rear entrance in case of fire.

Life on the campgrounds was simple, centering around the daily religious services, prayer meetings, and exhortations, all attended by bewhiskered men in their suits, women with their hoops and bustles, and occasionally children. Between the religious meetings, there was a constant hub of activity — people socializing, women preparing food, men and boys carrying water from nearby Squash Meadow Pond or gathering wood for the cooking fires, girls filling the bed ticks with fresh straw, children running and playing, and people going for a welcome dip in the ocean.

At night, people retired to their tents for their final prayers, many of them sleeping either on the ground, or if they were fortunate, on wooden tent floors covered with straw and under light blankets or quilts. The evenings were quiet except for the hushed whispers from neighboring tents. Stars blinked through the canopy of trees, and lights flickered from the lanterns in each tent.

When the five-year lease obtained upon the return to Wesleyan Grove expired in 1850, Sirson Coffin, son of one of the founders of the first camp-meeting, arranged for an eleven-year lease at $30 per year. He also signed two additional leases for lands adjacent to the premises for another $6. The area now encompassed between twelve and fifteen acres.

The long-term lease promoted the idea of permanent improvements to the grounds. More people of high standing and wealth were attending the camp-meetings, and commercial enterprises — washerwomen, bootblacks, bake tents, meat and vegetable carts — started to appear to serve them. Transportation became easier as entrepreneurs offered horse-drawn carts for passengers and wagons to haul trunks. Taking this even a step further, a Committee of Conveyance was appointed in 1864 to arrange travel for persons and baggage. New wells were ordered dug in 1849 and 1858, and shade trees were planted to replace some of the oaks whose top branches were dying. Plans for new seating and preachers' stand were made. Finally, the main circle was enlarged in 1854 to make room for more society tents, which a year later had reached a total of fifty.

MVCMA collection

A family tent with deep overhang of canvas and planking on the ground to protect the long skirts from the dust or mud.

Growth also increased expenses, and a tax of fifty cents was ordered in 1856 for each tent to help defray the costs of the meetings.

Ministers, all representing various churches, formed the governing body of the camp-meetings. The Island ministers, the original organizers, were soon outnumbered by the mainland ministers, who quickly took control of the camp-meeting. Although the Island ministers felt pushed aside, peace prevailed.

During the next few years, the camp-meeting began to adopt more formal business procedures and to name committees, made up of laity and clergy, to facilitate the needs of the rapidly growing community. Although there had been rules issued daily from the preachers' stand since the first meeting in 1835, a formal set of rules and regulations was first adopted in 1853 and further amended in 1858. Joseph Chase Allen, reporting in the *Vineyard Gazette*, described the authors of the rules as "Methodist ministers of the old fashioned fanatical type, and the regulations were rigid indeed. No loud boisterous conversations, no drinking, no card-playing, decorous conduct between the sexes, and many other rules were enforced

An interior view of a family tent. The center curtains divide the tent into two sections, with the sleeping quarters with a bed in the back and the folding chairs in the front providing portable seating. Later the tents became much more elaborately decorated.

A view of John Alden's cottage at 413 Washington Park (now 30 Victorian Park). The people in the picture are members of the Carpenter, Warden, Farnham, and Alden families who were campground neighbors. This is one of the few one-story cottages remaining; it is easy to see how cottages replaced tents.

or let it be said, enforced as rigidly as possible."

Yet, even in more modern times of today, the rules have had a purpose. Rev. Dr. Mary Jane O'Connor Ropp, who was pastor of Trinity United Methodist Church from 2002 to 2007, once described the rules as "designed to make it a peaceful and harmonious place for everyone, not just for some. A healthy interdependence pervades campground life."

In 1856, the land occupied by the camp-meeting was sold to a Mr. Dykes of Wareham, who was demanding an exorbitant rent ($100) or sale price ($1,600) for the land. After refusing to accept the price, a camp-meeting committee was formed to select a new site. Later, the land was returned to the previous owners and in 1858 a new ten-year lease was negotiated with the right to renew and, if the property were ever to be sold, the right to purchase the grounds at market value.

According to Charles E. Banks, whose *History of Martha's Vineyard* (1911) has long been considered the definitive early history of the Vineyard, this new, long-term lease not only assured the permanency of the camp-meeting but also spurred the establishment of the Town of Oak Bluffs. Banks flatly declares, "This [the camp-meeting] was the inception of the settlement which afterwards became Oak Bluffs."

There is little doubt that the lease gave the camp-meeting leaders the confidence and security to make permanent improvements on the grounds. Members, for the first time, authorized the leaders to borrow $1,000 to make repairs and add to more permanent structures. Another new well was dug; since a single well had served some eight or ten thousand people and three hundred horses, it was always a wonder that no contamination had sickened anyone. The Association also agreed to use most of the borrowed funds to erect a large, two-and-a-half-story building for offices and storage.

Camp-meeting attendees also felt safe in adding to their investment on the grounds. New family tents were built or repaired, and several new large tents were placed in the circle. Some members even began to erect more enduring houses built of wood.

The camp-meeting at Wesleyan Grove had come far since its humble beginnings twenty-three years earlier. Attendance had grown from a few hundred attendees, most of them from the Vineyard, to 6,000 attending the Friday exercises in 1858 and over 12,000 attending the Sabbath, many of these traveling great distances.

There were now about sixty large tents in the main circle three to four times the size of the original nine, a large number of family tents/cottages, and several large boarding tents where simple foods were served. Overall, there were more than 320 structures, with sixty new sites being readied for the following year.

The grounds had grown from an acre to between twelve and fifteen acres. The number of ministers had grown from nineteen at the third meeting to over 100. They preached more than 500 sermons and oversaw 1,150 conversions.

A picniclike atmosphere was beginning to emerge, as people began to come early and stay late to enjoy the setting and the social opportunities.

A woman from Edgartown, commenting after the close of the camp-meeting, called it "the bestest camp-meeting I've ever attended," and added, "I thank the Lord that in eleven months and a fortnight we will have another."

The first cottage in Wesleyan Grove was built in 1856 for Rev. Frederick Upham on Upham's Hill (now Cottage Park). It was a seven-by-ten-foot, one-room wooden structure that was later incorporated into the back of a larger cottage and eventually removed altogether.

Blessing God for Wooden Shingles

1859~1865

"Many thousands of persons visited the camp-meeting merely to enjoy a day's pleasures."

BOSTON ATLAS AND BEE, 1859

The camp-meeting at Wesleyan Grove was becoming the largest and most famous of all the camp-meetings. At a time when the entire population of the Island was just over 4,000, more than 5,000 people thronged the grove daily in the summer of 1859. And over 12,000 came on Camp-Meeting Sunday.

Many of those had heard about the fiery evangelical spirit of the camp-meeting and came to see it for themselves. For those who attended more formal and somber services in traditional churches, including other denominations, it was quite a sight: thundering assaults upon sin from the pulpits, women weeping and fainting, hands raised to the Lord, loud shouts of praise, lost souls coming forward to be saved, beautiful hymn singing.

Others came for pure pleasure. A reporter from the *Boston Atlas and Bee* described a scene far removed from the more serious days of the early camp: "Everybody appeared happy, joyful, smiling; thousands of young and beautiful females, elegantly dressed, promenaded along green paths with young men, whilst an immense crowd listened attentively to eloquent and deeply impressive addresses from clergymen, whose only object appeared to be to save souls."

As Hebron Vincent said, "People came of different denominations and of no denominations; and so long as they were decorous, as were almost all those who came, we heartily welcomed them, and were happy to have them mingle with us in our social circles, and in our religious devotions."

People met at the water pumps, going to and from services, or just walking on the narrow pathways on the grounds. It was not uncommon for people to meet at tent openings dressed in a casual manner and to think nothing of it. Women made tea or coffee while socializing with friends; men played croquet or sat engaged in conversation; children played games.

The need for more substantial accommodations continued to increase. Temporary tents were giving way to wooden cottages, and a building era that lasted twenty-six years began with the construction of the Association Building in 1859. Most of the cottages were constructed between 1859 and 1880, Trinity Methodist Church in 1878, the Tabernacle in 1879, and Grace Chapel in 1885.

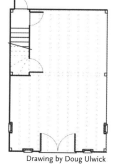

Drawing by Doug Ulwick

The typical Martha's Vineyard Campground Cottage is built of yellow pine tongue and groove vertical boarding. It is eleven to sixteen feet wide and one-and-a-half stories high. The height of the steeply pitched roof is usually twice the cottage width. All the cottages today have been modified — porch roofs were added in the 1880s, and kitchens and bathrooms became common in the early 1900s.

T he desire for comfort probably led to the more enduring houses built of wood, a trend that accelerated after 1858. The transition from the tents to the permanent homes was gradual. The first step had been above-ground platforms for the tents that prevented inhabitants from getting wet during rainstorms. Then wooden frames made it easier to set up and support the canvas tents. Wooden sides better protected the inhabitants and the contents from heavy winds. Finally, the roof was the ultimate protection. The move away from tents accelerated during the Civil War, when the cost of canvas became prohibitively high.

The first wooden cottage, a simple one-room structure, was built for Rev. Frederick Upham on Upham's Hill (now Cottage Park) in 1856. After a particularly severe rainstorm one night that blew down many tents, Rev. Upham exclaimed as he emerged from his wooden tent wearing dry clothes, "Bless God for shingles!"

The early wooden structures were built by the tent/cottage owners themselves. As the structures became more substantial, builders (primarily from Edgartown and New Bedford), and sometimes architects, became involved. Many Islanders who were shipbuilders turned to house construction when the whaling industry declined after the discovery of oil in 1859. What emerged was an all-new architectural form some refer to as Carpenter's Gothic and what has become known as the Martha's Vineyard Campground Cottage. The cost of the cottages ranged from $100 to $700 with the most expensive one (10 Trinity Park) built for Governor and later U.S. Senator William Sprague IV of Rhode Island at a cost of $3,500 in 1869. Furnishings were eclectic, from simple and modest to luxurious ones befitting a city drawing room.

It is still disputed which was the first cottage of substance to be built. Some believe it was the

Perez Mason, architect of the campgrounds

Doug Ulwick collection

The Mason/Lawton cottage was built in 1860 for the Perez Mason and William Lawton families. Designed by Perez Mason, it was built in Warren, Rhode Island, shipped to the Vineyard in pieces, and assembled on the present location (70 Trinity Park). The people shown in the picture are probably members of those families.

PEREZ MASON, a well-known architect from Providence, Rhode Island, was a campground resident and certainly influenced the look of the area. He designed the Association Office building, built in 1859 for $1,000, and probably the cottage next door, which was later pushed back and turned on the lot and ultimately lost in the fire of 1973. That cottage is thought to have been the first cottage of substance. Many of the architectural features may be similar to those found on the Association Building.

The Mason/Lawton Cottage, mentioned by Hebron Vincent in 1860 (70 Trinity Park), was designed by Mason and built for his family and the family of William B. Lawton. Designed as a duplex, it was shipped to the Vineyard in pieces, and assembled at the chosen location where it stands today. Each side has three rooms on the ground floor and a stairway leading to the upper sleeping quarters. Both families shared the cottage for many years until Mason designed and built his tower cottage on Clinton Avenue. Unfortunately, the only remains of this tower cottage are in photographs.

In 1861, he designed the new preachers' stand and new seating that provided accommodations for as many as three to four thousand people.

An interior view of the larger addition made to the Sarah Cook Cottage at 79 Trinity Park. Note the high level of finishings and the fancy trim over the two doors leading into different rooms, with an unseen stairway in the center of the cottage.

Mason/Lawton Cottage (70 Trinity Park), mentioned in 1860 as "the most costly and beautiful" of the homes. The two-family pre-fab cottage was shipped to the Island in pieces from Warren, Rhode Island, and reassembled at the head of Trinity Park. Another contender, according to *Martha's Vineyard, A Short History and Guide*, published in 1956 and edited by Eleanor R. Mayhew, is a cottage built in 1859 that sat on the right next to the Association Building as you entered Trinity Park. There is photographic evidence indicating the cottage might have been pushed back and turned on the lot at some point and attached to a larger cottage (79 Trinity Park) built in front on the same lot facing the Tabernacle. If that is correct, the original section was destroyed by the fire in 1973.

As the encampment continued to grow, the layout of the meeting grounds changed to make room for additional society tents and wooden homes in the main circle and for avenues and pathways. A forty-foot-wide avenue named Asbury Avenue (later called Broadway and now Trinity Park) was laid out in 1859 and encompassed the entire circle of about forty society tents. To make room for additional smaller tents, the area on the other side of the road was cleared and several small avenues, such as Fisk Avenue, were laid out, as was a triangular area on the southern part of the encampment, now part of Trinity Park.

The encampment was again enlarged in 1864 to the south (probably Forest and Rural circles), to accommodate hundreds of tents and cottages; this new area was large enough to hold a more traditionally sized camp-meeting. A year later, the grounds included about twenty-six acres with avenues of about five hundred tents and forty wooden houses, with an additional hundred lots ready for the following year.

Several of the areas were established by people affiliated with the same church, and the areas they inhabited were named after their church to reflect that. County Park's inhabitants were members of the County Street Church in New Bedford; Allen Avenue and Fourth Street Avenue were both named after churches in New Bedford. Other areas were formed by groups of friends or families who arranged their tents in ways that encouraged sociability. Pease Avenue was named for five Edgartown Peases who pitched their tents in that area, including relatives of original founder Jeremiah Pease.

Eventually, there were over six hundred cottages located on the campgrounds. Today there are 314; the number dwindled as some of the cottages were joined together to form more substantial homes. Others fell into disrepair or were moved. Moving cottages was quite common during those early years: with lightweight construction and no plumbing or electrical wiring, it was easy. Even as late as the 1950s, cottages were being moved within the campgrounds to more favorable locations or even off the grounds to larger lots or to avoid the restrictions of the Association rules.

Grace Frey, a lifelong resident of Oak Bluffs, tells of Judge Herbert M. Chase, who was the owner of the Wesley House, who moved five cottages to Winemack Avenue in the 1930s to make room for a parking lot. The Crystal Palace at 45 Pequot Avenue, Windswept across from the Martha's Vineyard Hospital, 3 Martha's Park Road in Hart Haven, and the two cottages remaining at 14 and 10 Winemack are examples of those moved off the campgrounds.

Many expressed concern that the ambiance of the camp-meeting was being lost as more wooden structures emerged. They felt the romantic time of the old days was disappearing — the smell of the straw on which they slept, the lanterns that remained lit all night, the buckets of water that were kept at ready by the tent door in case of fire, and most of all, being lulled to sleep by the wind rustling through the trees. But, as one reporter stated, "The snug warm cottages prevailed, as manifest destiny decreed that they should."

The camp-meeting was now village-like, and commercial tents increased to meet the varied needs of the crowds — adding barbers, photographers, refreshment stands, a post office, and tents providing useful and sanitary purposes. There were about fifteen licensed boarding tents ranging from pay-to-grab fare — the early version of fast food — to fairly elaborate menus with seating for fifty to four hundred and sometimes replenishing and refilling several times at one meal.

Tents had patented whale oil lamps, and streetlights were installed along the avenues for $106 in 1863. New wells were dug, and each year several young trees were planted in an attempt to replenish oaks damaged by throngs trampling on the grounds.

A new preachers' stand and new seating added in 1861 at a cost of $1,500 were far grander than the

Harvey Garneau Jr. collection

A group of ministers is gathered at the aptly named preachers' stand sometime before 1869.

original ones built in 1835 and 1846. The new seats reached all the way to the preachers' stand and seated three to four thousand. To make them more comfortable, the new seats were built with backs, a much heralded improvement. A large bell that was nicknamed Ezekiel stood by the preachers' stand to help preserve order. It was used to announce the hours of public services, early prayer meetings, tent meetings, and the summons for rising in the morning and retiring at night.

The *Camp-Meeting Herald*, believed by Hebron Vincent to be the first journal of its kind ever printed, was first published daily during the camp-meeting in 1862. The spicy and interesting articles about the activities on the campgrounds were popular, and issues sold rapidly.

To make sure these improvements were not wasted, the grove occupied by the camp-meeting for thirty years was purchased in 1865 for $1,300. With the responsibility for land, thousands of people, and a growing infrastructure, Agent Coffin recommended the formation of a new organization of laymen to handle the business affairs of the camp-meetings, leaving the ministers to oversee religious matters. Under the new system, the agent, whose responsibility was the care and management of the grounds, a finance

People gathered for religious services in front of the preachers' stand designed by Perez Mason and erected in 1861. Seating between thirty and forty persons, the stand was a five-sided shape of an octagon with a straight closed back, about twenty feet in length with open sides and a roof projecting six feet each way. A slightly elevated platform in front was enclosed by a railing where singers sat or where anxious persons could come forward for prayer. Note the wood-backed benches.

The State Police began to maintain order on the campgrounds in 1865. Their headquarters were located on Broadway (now Trinity Park) sometime after the Civil War. The gentleman on the far left is Capt. Robert Crossman, great-great-grandfather of Don Andrew of East Chop.

committee, and a treasurer began to meet on a regular basis. To herald this new permanency, eleven articles of agreement were drawn up and adopted in 1860, with Article I fixing the name of the association as the Martha's Vineyard Camp-Meeting Association (MVCMA).

Vigilant volunteers helped keep order on the grounds. One reporter commented that with "the many thousands in their tents or promenading along the avenues at one time … this was the most quiet and orderly religious convocation ever seen."

But, as with anywhere, there were always those who tried to break the rules. Fifteen or more gallons of liquor were found secreted in the woods in 1862. Other parcels of liquor were found at various secluded places or detected on the shore, and the liquor was destroyed to avert "other forms of evil" and to make sure it didn't cause "crazing effects upon some who were their ready patrons."

The clouds of Civil War shadowed the camp-meetings of 1861–1865, and there were strong feelings about slavery. The concerns about slavery had shown up at the camp-meeting as early as 1844 when an appeal was made on behalf of a "good colored sister" who was asking for money to purchase her son from slavery. Fifty dollars was requested and sixty was raised, although several times that sum was needed. The ministers often called for prayers for the soldiers and expressed hopes that they could observe the Sabbath.

Despite concerns that attendance would decline during the war years, the camp-meeting continued to grow. An estimated 10,000 were on the grounds on the Sabbath during 1863 and 1864. At the end of the war thousands came from the whole eastern United States and beyond, many aboard the steamer *Monohansett* when it was returned from government service. Other boats, including *Eagle's Wing* and *Island Home*, plus a fleet of other steamers and sailing vessels moved back and forth between the mainland and the Vineyard.

The hubbub created such a festive spirit that it could not be suppressed by the frowns of some elders. People were coming earlier, including the ministers, to set up their personal accommodations and to enjoy themselves.

By the end of the Civil War, many families were staying the entire month of August. Although Vincent supported the change because he felt it was "a good thing for people to dwell beneath the shade of the grand old oaks for a few weeks," others were not happy with the trend.

They feared the religious character of the campgrounds was waning, and that an earnest effort needed to be made to revive the old standards. Prayer meetings were increased to as many as thirty-six a day, and more sermons, exhortations, and hymn sings were added.

Although there were complaints of too many religious exercises, others felt the general character of the meeting was decidedly better than it had been the past few years.

Yet not much could turn back the clock: the camp-meeting was taking on the characteristics of an organized and well-run community, and was in fact becoming a summer resort. At the close of the meeting in 1865, Vincent wrote, "Could the fathers, who preached in the camp-meeting held in Wesleyan Grove some thirty years ago revisit the place now, they would hardly be able to identify the spot, except from the surroundings, which was then so consecrated and hallowed."

Filigree

MVCMA collection

Hebron Vincent refers to this cottage in an article written in 1872 as one of the first of artistic ambition. Thought to be designed by Perez Mason, it was built for Mrs. Sarah A. Cook and later turned and pushed back to face Washington Avenue (now Butler Avenue) to make way for the attachment of a larger cottage built in 1879 that faced the Tabernacle (79 Trinity Park). The pictured cottage was destroyed by fire in 1973.

UNTIL 1871, the decorative filigree on the cottages was probably winter work for builders in Edgartown who owned jigsaws. In that year, the Fisher and Huxford planing mill was built next to the new Highland Wharf north of the campgrounds to produce tongue-and-groove planed boards, rough and planed joints, cottage frames and shingles, and jigsaw trim. They were joined in 1880 by the Cottage City Novelty Works, which did complete cottage construction and jigsaw trim. A recently discovered stereoview indicates the presence of a mill owned by John S. Hammond, designer and manufacturer of cottage trimmings at Vineyard Grove, Martha's Vineyard.

The factories were kept busy with orders as people decorated their cottages with a variety of vergeboard and balcony trims — even the staid Methodists. The trim added a dainty and festive air to the cottages that gave Oak Bluffs its old name of Cottage City.

The Providence House, once located in Montgomery Square and mentioned by Hebron Vincent as the first boarding/lodging establishment of substance, was built in 1865. Meals were served on the ground floor with lodging on the second.

An early view of Trinity Park, probably then called Asbury Street or Broadway Avenue. The trolley tracks, laid prior to the 1873 season, run in front of a row of single-story tents and cottages. The grounds already have a clearly laid-out, residential feel.

Missed Opportunity

1866~1867

"Is it a reality? Am I really in the old Wesleyan Grove? Or am I in some fairy-land?"

REV. HEBRON VINCENT

After the Civil War, life in the United States began to undergo a revolution fueled by industry and technology: the telephone and telegraph, the electric light and electric motor, central heating and indoor plumbing, the transcontinental railroad and transatlantic cable, large corporations, and mass production. With transportation affordable and cities crowded with factories and people, many began to take time for rest and recreation.

Returning to their summer retreat on the Vineyard brought them to a place where tents and new cottages under stately oaks were the only things that broke up the open fields of the sheep pasture. For thirty-one years, this camp-meeting had afforded them peaceful solitude, and the first view of their beloved grounds made the difficult trek well worth the effort. But life was becoming far more crowded even here.

Two weeks before the camp-meeting of 1866, sixty carpenters and painters worked from dawn to dusk erecting and beautifying cottages, which now cost from $200 to $700. Fifty cottages had already been constructed that year, and by the end of the year there would be over 600 tents/cottages on the grounds. Changes to the grounds had made room for new structures, and business establishments were open and ready for the new season. More land had been purchased, bringing the total camp-meeting site to thirty-five acres, and a new wharf built with a new road, Kedron Avenue (now New York Avenue), that led to the grove.

Steamers arrived daily bringing building supplies, baggage, and people. One hundred families arrived early and were preparing their sites, greeting old friends, walking in the fields and along the cliffs, swimming, and enjoying other recreations. There were daily religious services, prayer meetings, and hymn sings.

The Oak Bluffs Land and Wharf Company's wharf and first hotel, probably taken from the Pawnee House on Kennebec Avenue. To make room for the Sea View House built in 1872, this small hotel was later moved, in two parts, to Circuit Avenue and reassembled to form the Island House.

Dagnall/Tucker collection

Partnerships

Doug Ulwick collection

The Union Chapel, built by the Oak Bluffs Land and Wharf Company in 1870 at a cost of $16,000, was the first of three major houses of worship constructed. A short-lived bell tower is shown.

THE SIX MEN who started the Oak Bluffs Land and Wharf Company came from different backgrounds. The six partners, who all had equal shares, were:

✻ Captain Shubael L. Norton, who acquired the land after the division of the estate of William Butler, who had first allowed the camp-meeting to take place on his sheep pasture,
✻ Captain Ira Darrow, master of a packet plying between the Vineyard and the mainland and owner of a coal yard,
✻ Captain Grafton Norton Collins, former master of the whaleship Walter Scott,
✻ William Bradley, a storekeeper and bank director,
✻ William S. Hill of Boston, a former merchant,
✻ Erastus Payson Carpenter, a businessman from Foxboro, Massachusetts.

All but Hill and Carpenter were from Edgartown.

An annoying incident *as described by Hebron Vincent*

"IT WAS REPORTED that during a Sabbath evening service in 1865, a large fleet of yachts, said to have been from New York, had been spending some time in this vicinity. On the Sabbath evening, while they were lying in the harbor nearby, there was fired from them a succession of heavy guns, occupying a considerable portion of the time of preaching, greatly annoying the worshipers. The hour of public worship must have been known. Thus to annoy a large gathering of Christian worshipers was unprincipled, to do it on a Sabbath evening was impiety. The yachtsmen were probably of the more wealthy, as usual, and doubtless claim to be gentlemen. But, in the judgment of candor, the act, uncalled for as it was, was as ungentlemanly as it was unchristian."

The elaborate cottages and old oak trees along Trinity Park provide a tranquil place to retreat. Houses were so close together that polite rules grew up to protect residents' privacy.

Although the early campgrounders came in the hot summer months, they did not compromise in their formal and heavy clothing. Note the Romanesque rounded arch of the doorway and windows.

A gothic cottage on Clinton Avenue included an elaborately draped flag awning. Cottage owners were proud of individualizing their summer homes.

An early view of Fourth Street Avenue, lined with tents and cottages, looking toward Domestic Square (later Commonwealth Square).

A week before the meeting, people numbered in the thousands, and a reported 12,000 visited the grounds during camp-meeting week. Some who came only out of curiosity were so taken with the atmosphere that they wanted to stay, only to find that no lots were available on the campgrounds. Land adjacent to the campground had been used for temporary commercial shelters and private tents. Since newcomers were eager to buy more lots, the owner of the approximately seventy-five acres, Captain Shubael L. Norton of Edgartown, offered the land to the Association. The property included all the open land between the campground and the beach, the beach itself, and the bluffs southeast of the lake.

Association members hesitated over the purchase; they still had areas of undeveloped land from two recent purchases, and they would need to raise the additional $3,000 that Norton wanted for the land. Others felt they had begun to stray too far from the original purpose and were against further expansion — and still others found it hard to believe that anyone else would want to live in or visit the area if they were not coming to the camp-meetings. They believed the area was still too isolated and difficult to reach.

If the Association did not see the commercial value of the land, others did. They had seen the number of people who came and the vacation-like atmosphere they brought. Norton and whaling Captain Ira Darrow of Edgartown had years earlier built the beach bathhouses used by campgrounders and had attended some of the camp-meetings. They and others they showed the property to saw the opportunity for a profitable investment and took advantage of it, just as a *Boston Courier* newspaper reporter predicted in 1860 when he wrote, "Some

enterprising men will make princely fortunes here, in purchasing lands, soon to be in demand."

The Association's hesitation had huge consequences. The board was still deliberating when Captain Norton sold five shares of the land — maintaining a sixth for himself — to a group of investors who had made their fortunes and were looking for a post war economic venture.

The investors pooled their resources and formed the Oak Bluffs Land and Wharf Company (OBC or the Company).

The six partners included Erastus P. Carpenter, a successful businessman who set the new company in motion with his promotional and business abilities. Within the year, the area today known as the Copeland District was laid out in small residential lots, curved avenues, and park areas designed by Boston landscape artist Robert Morris Copeland. The Company built a substantial wharf (where the Steamship Authority wharf is today) for about $5,000. A large, one-and-a-half-story building for storage, meals, and rental lodging was constructed at the head of the wharf. (That building was later moved in two pieces to Circuit Avenue, to make room for the Sea View Hotel; it now houses the Island House.) By the end of the year, several lots were sold and three cottages completed in the new planned community, one of them an elaborate home for Carpenter.

Many of the cottages in the new resort mimicked those being built in the campgrounds, though the costs for the resort housing were substantially higher. While cottages in the campgrounds ranged in price from $400 to $1,500, the ones in the new resort ran from $750 to $4,000.

Early celebrations of Illumination Night called for elaborate preparation, obvious in this flag-decked tent. Japanese lanterns also decorate both the outside and inside of the tent.

A view of Central House, originally named Dunbar House and later the Beatrice House, and bakery, both along Central Avenue on the left. The thirty-one-room building was built in 1866 for somewhere between $2,000 and $3,000. It became the sixty-room Central House in 1879.

Later, many of these original small cottages in the resort were replaced by larger and more elaborate ones.

Campgrounders eyed the nearby development nervously, while rumors flew that the Company's intentions were hostile to the religious purpose of the camp-meeting. Others felt the camp-meeting itself should find another location. Recognizing it had made a mistake, the Association unsuccessfully tried to buy the land from the new owners.

A series of meetings between members of both organizations between August 1866 and April 1867 ended with a measure of harmony. Each side recognized it had invested heavily in its respective grounds. Company leaders assured the Association that their business would not conflict with the interests of the camp-meeting and agreed to sell or lease all lots subject to the restrictions and regulations of the Association during the time of camp-meeting. Reassured, the Association gave up the idea of moving to a different location.

Stannard/Riedinger collection

The Association was also given free use of the new wharf and was deeded half an acre of land, now located near Nancy's Snack Bar, to straighten out the boundary line between the two properties. A historian later would write that the campground management accepted the land with thanks and showed their "appreciation" by immediately using the new acquisition for a colony of public outhouses.

This reflected the resentment harbored by some, as Hebron Vincent described it, "that gentlemen whose contiguous lands would never have been worth a tithe of their purchase money but for this religious meeting, should avail themselves of the opportunity to plant by their side a large interest so diverse in its nature and object."

The formation of the Company forced the MVCMA to face reality: The distractions and pleasures of the modern world were surrounding its refuge. Yet despite concern that attendance would decrease with the arrival of the Company, there were somewhere between 1,200 and 1,500 people on the grounds in the week before the camp-meeting of 1867. Crowds continued to come, the religious services were well-attended, enthusiasm was high, and business was as usual.

The Company was good to its word. All activities of recreation were ordered to cease for the week of camp-meeting. The sanctity of the Sabbath was observed on and off the campgrounds. Boats were anchored away from the pier, no carriages were running, and all but essential places of business were closed. Ultimately, the MVCMA and the OBC together formed a unique community from which the Town of Oak Bluffs grew — a friendly, interdependent community with many of today's inhabitants being descendants of the early campgrounders, commercial entrepreneurs, and resort residents.

The Frasier House, Oak Bluffs, Mass.

The Frasier Cottage (facing page) in an early view without the third-floor addition, and later with the addition (above). It operated on the American Plan (meals included), and was located at the intersection of Fourth Avenue and Trinity Park. The lobby, dining room, and kitchen were all on the first floor, and rooms with shared baths were on the second and third floors.

The Wesley House in Commonwealth Square before the addition of the fourth floor. Note the barber pole on the left and the Howard House in the foreground, which later became part of the Wesley House.

A view of Everett House looking toward the entrance to County Park (now Wesleyan Grove). The boarding/lodging house faces into Montgomery Square with Central Avenue on the right. The dining room seated one hundred guests and cottagers and provided rooms accommodating fifty.

A wedding being held at the preachers' stand with musical accompaniment provided by the melodeon in front of the stand. Note the bride's attendants on the right holding flowers and the groom's attendants on the left. The lanterns on the poles provided light for evening services.

A Seaside Resort Emerges
1868~1869

"The climate is delightful, and the proximity to the sea renders bathing, fishing and sailing easily accessible."

BOSTON SEMI-WEEKLY ADVISER 1868

The two communities, though side by side, were something of a dichotomy — the peace and tranquility under the oaks in the campgrounds, and the vibrant and festive air of the resort only a few yards away. One historian years later said, "Inside the campground all was neighborly and hushed. Outside, quite suddenly all was clamor and commerce — a town of skating rinks, merry-go-rounds, theaters, and hotels."

In the weeks leading up to the camp-meeting, the Association was preparing the grounds, while many who had arrived early were readying tents and building and furnishing new cottages. The businesses on the campgrounds were setting up and providing goods and services. At the same time, the OBC was laying out lots in anticipation of sales and building new structures for its new resort.

People in both places were enjoying themselves. The game of croquet became so popular on the campgrounds that both the clergy and their flock were chastised for being late to services, and a resolution prohibiting the game within the main circle was passed in 1868.

With no shower facilities and plenty of summer heat, sea bathing was a popular activity for all, even in the heavy bathing costumes of the day. To avoid the uncomfortable walk back to their tents/cottages, many rented beach bathhouses owned by the OBC's Darrow and Norton to change into their bathing costumes.

Clearly, people had begun to think of this as a place for more than fiery preaching: The marriage of Adin B. Capron and Miss Irene Ballou of Woonsocket, Rhode Island, took place on August 9, 1869, prior to the camp-meeting. The *Vineyard Gazette* reported that the preachers' stand was decorated with American flags and flowers and 1,500 people witnessed it, some climbing trees to see.

A view of Montgomery Square showing the Beatrice House (formerly the Central House), the Arcade built by the OBC, and a German American Bakery (at one time Coyle Brothers Ideal Bakery). There is a bakery attached to the Beatrice House and a photographer's studio just beyond. Other business establishments in the square include J. J. Costigan the Vineyard Taylor (#22), Hammonds Market (#4), the Everett and Providence Houses, H. W. DeCorsey's Barbership (#3), and a New York Store for millinery, boots, and shoes.

Boarding establishments

AT ONE TIME, the MVCMA boasted of several large boarding/lodging establishments on its grounds. The first boarding tent, called the Providence House, was built in 1865 in Montgomery Square. The cottage at 20 Lincoln Avenue served as its horse stable, with domestic servant lodging provided on the second floor. Others followed: the Beatrice House, the Everett House, the Frazier House, the Vineyard Grove House, and the Attleboro and Wesley houses.

The only two surviving establishments are the Attleboro House and the Wesley House.

Businesses had quickly grown up to serve the thousands of people flocking to the camp-meeting site, and then to the new resort. Here, one of the many vendors' tents probably located in one of the three main commercial areas offers hot tea and coffee.

Recreational activities became part of everyday life on the campgrounds including such activities as archery, bicycling, croquet, sailing, and swimming.

Songs from a melodeon played as the happy couple embarked on the steamer *Helen Augusta* — the bride wearing a handsome traveling suit of steel gray.

Circuit Avenue was only budding as a commercial area, and businesses were primarily located on the outskirts of the campgrounds. It was common for the businesses to be moved to accommodate the increasing number of tents/cottages and to make room for the addition of avenues and streets. Ultimately, the commercial establishments were concentrated in three main locations — Montgomery Square near the arcade entrance to the campgrounds, Commonwealth Square at the back entrance of the Wesley House, and at the foot of School Street where Tabernacle House is located today.

New buildings and constant changes continued to bring increased commercial ventures to the area. The merchants were wide ranging in their offerings: An ad announcing the grand opening of a ladies hair dressing parlor appeared in 1870 offering visitors a chance to have their hair "frizzed, curled, permed, and chignoned to the latest style of the art." Boarding and lodging establishments, bakeries, milliners, tailors, photographers' studios, markets, barbershops, drugstores, furniture stores, fancy crockery, refresh-

Glass collection

Harvey Garneau Jr. collection

Roque — a bumper pool version of croquet (top photo) — and children's games provided moments of pleasure between religious services and chores.

ment stands, and more could be found. There was also a post office, a newspaper office, a laundry, a hardware store, and a lumber yard.

Bazaars were set up along the long plank walk that ran from the Highland Wharf by the lakeside where various souvenirs were for sale, including those made from shells or clay from the Gay Head cliffs.

Licensed vendors also sold a wide range of wares from door to door. Camp-meeting attendees could buy ice cream with musical coronet accompaniment played by the vendor, have knives sharpened, or purchase a "camp meetinger" cap, fresh flowers, fruits and vegetables, or a 250-page Turkish-bound Morocco book showing more than twenty pictures of the campgrounds.

Although peddlers were not generally allowed on the campgrounds, they were sometimes willing to take a chance. One merchant sold fresh produce from his cart while singing Methodist revival hymns in hopes of attracting business. Another traveled with his donkey and cart selling straw for bed ticks and milk from his goats. After the camp-meeting was over he gathered the used straw to feed his donkeys during the winter, and if he was lucky he might find a few loose coins.

A view of Domestic Square (now Commonwealth Square) filled with activity. Vendors offered everything from popcorn to furnishings for tents/cottages. More formal businesses, like the Wesley and Howard houses and Dr. Leach's Drug Store, replaced the temporary buildings.

Lake Avenue looking into Commonwealth Square. On the left is Howard House, advertising nonalcoholic Ottawa Beer. One Commonwealth Square, on the right, housed the Cottage City Star newspaper and served as a year-round church meeting place before Trinity Methodist Church was built.

An electric car circa 1908. The candles on the ground were in preparation for Grand Illumination.

Outside the "charmed circle"

A REPORTER for the *Boston Semi-Weekly Advertiser* described the area in 1869 as follows: "The climate is delightful, and the proximity to the sea renders bathing, fishing and sailing easily accessible. Many of the people take their servants and have their food prepared in their own houses, the markets and the provision stores being furnished with all the luxuries of the season. There are several restaurants where board can be obtained for those who prefer this method of living. Among the important additions made this past season is a beanery, which … has become an absolute necessity." He estimated that 387 quarts of beans and 421 loaves of brown bread were sold on one Saturday.

The cottages take shape

Doug Ulwick collection

Elaborate cottages with wide front porches or steps offered perfect lounging spots during camp-meeting.

ONE OBSERVER described the cottages, which then numbered about five hundred, as follows: "The best in style are what may be called American Carpenter's Renaissance with dainty, light balconies, piazzas, ornamented windows and Venetian blinds, a pretty style on the whole and admirably adapted to its transitory uses. Each cottage of the better class has a front or rear space devoted to flowers or decorated with sea shells, wild vines, honeysuckles, classical vases, and even sculptures. Oriental furniture is very common on balconies, while everywhere are the latest appliances for comfortable lounging and rocking which Yankee ingenuity has invented."

Not everyone agreed. One dissenter wrote home telling of those "gothic shanties" and referred with distaste to the "queer and profane architecture."

Then there were the stories you don't want to hear. This same entrepreneur collected discarded food bits from the boarding tents which his wife then used to make the best mincemeat in town.

Business flourished.

The grounds of both organizations resounded with building activity and preparations for the arriving crowds. In the campgrounds, cottages were appearing as if by magic, produced by the fifty or sixty carpenters constantly at work. By the end of 1869, there were about 200 cottages, with prices now ranging from $400 to $1,500, and approximately 700 tents and cottage tents made of board and sailcloth. An ice house, built for $1,000 by the MVCMA, was constructed to provide a source of income.

Even with the purchase of an additional three acres in 1869, now bringing the total to more than thirty-eight acres, the MVCMA was running out of room to expand. As a result, a restriction was made limiting to one the number of lots an owner could lease, with the exception of lots located in the rear used for cooking purposes and those lots leased for double buildings.

To help maintain order, all tent/cottage owners were responsible for the conduct of anyone occupying the tent/cottage. Any violation of rules or conditions of the lease would result in forfeiture of the lease and the immediate closing of the tent or cottage. Those wishing to rent their lots had to give the Association first refusal and provide the names and addresses of the renters.

Lowe collection

With the campground encampment filling up to capacity, people wishing to build a cottage, to own the land their cottages were built on, or desiring larger lots and cottages looked for locations on both sides of the MVCMA encampment.

The OBC had shown great enterprise. Eighty feet had been added to their wharf, making it 320 feet long and substantial enough to weather the winter ice and storms. An ad placed in the July 5, 1867, *Vineyard Gazette* promised a "Home by the Seaside, Oak Bluffs, A New Summer Resort." By the end of 1869, some three hundred lots had been sold.

The Town of Edgartown, realizing the growing value of the resort, placed a tax valuation of $15,000 on the area. (The campground itself, incorporated on May 1, 1868, was granted a tax exemption for twenty acres used for religious purposes, and Edgartown assessed the MVCMA a tax of $800 on the rest of the land.)

On the Saturday evening preceding the commencement of the camp-meeting of 1869, the OBC orchestrated a Grand Illumination night. Newly constructed cottages were decorated with Oriental lanterns, and the Foxboro Brass Band was hired to parade around the area and give a concert in the park. The evening ended with a beautiful display of fireworks. This illumination was probably a promotional event to entice people to purchase lots in the new development, but it would later be the first of many Grand Illumination nights that now take place only on the MVCMA grounds.

Cottages not only housed campground residents; they also served as places for commercial enterprises, as both the photo above of a bakery and the one on the facing page of the same house show.

A horse-drawn trolley in front of the Association Building moved campgrounders in comfort. The route at that time was a clockwise one through the grounds.

W. Douglas Thompson collection

The area before the canvas tent was erected for the season. The three center poles were fifty feet high and a foot and one half in diameter. During the season, the center pole would be topped by a white flag with a red Christian cross.

But notwithstanding the entertainment, which thousands attended, Hebron Vincent reported that two well-attended prayer meetings were held on the campgrounds at the same time.

With the construction of the New York Landing in 1865, people were approaching the campgrounds via what is now Lake Avenue. Clinton Avenue, the main entrance from the west, was transformed into a seventy-foot-wide avenue bordered by two rows of beautiful cottages, with walkways for the promenading crowds on either side of a wide grassy area. A new entrance was made along the pond shore coming in by the lumber yard (at the foot of Dukes County Avenue) on Siloam Avenue.

The parks, streets, and avenues were lit with petroleum oil lamps placed about one hundred feet apart. The lampposts were made of wood, turned, sanded and painted similar to those in the streets of Brooklyn, New York. The encampment was a magnificent sight to see with the light shining from the many lanterns which dotted the grounds.

For many years the oak trees that had so well protected the congregation from the elements had been losing their foliage or succumbing to the throngs trampling through the grounds. Since the trees no longer protected the attendees, a new canvas shelter, the precursor of today's iron tabernacle, was constructed.

Six thousand people were within the circle to hear the sermon on the Sabbath in 1868. About 4,000 people were residing upon the grounds during the summer, and another 30,000 visited the grounds during the summer months. More than 100 clergymen of different denominations took part in services at the stand or held services at various outposts to accommodate the vast crowds; many old-timers felt that this was the best season. Yet neither comfortable cottages, ample provisions nor people coming simply for "relaxation from business" affected the religious work of the camp-meeting grounds. The meeting that August seemed to lay aside fears about the development of the nearby resort.

Some still had reservations as to whether the campgrounds could comfortably live with the emerging resort. This, coupled with the fact that the MVCMA was running out of space to expand, moved some concerned members of the Association, acting independently, to purchase fifty-five acres of land northwest of the campgrounds in 1869. The area was covered with reindeer moss, occasional small groves of scrubby pines and oaks, and clumps of huckleberry and bayberry bushes. The parcel was more elevated than any of the neighboring lands, and was to be known as "The Vineyard Highlands."

The buyers' hopes were that it would be annexed to the encampment or, if necessary, be a place where the Association could move to escape the intrusion and influence of the OBC. Eventually, they would incorporate as the Vineyard Grove Company (VGC) following the refusal of the Association, in 1868, to pay $5,000 for the fifty-five acres.

The MVCMA that existed by the end of 1869 was, in many ways, the campgrounds of today: a friendly and active community of families that retained a sense of peace and tranquility, with a neighbor whose character was substantially different.

The layout of the grounds, the "gingerbread cottages," the length of the season — July and August, with many families arriving in June and remaining until mid-October — the religious services and Camp-Meeting Week, the board of directors conducting the business matters of the Association, and the lots leased to help defray the expenses, all still remain today.

The canvas tabernacle

THE PROTECTIVE CANVAS tabernacle referred to by Hebron Vincent as a "temporary awning" was erected in 1869 and used for ten seasons. It was made of 4,000 yards of sailcloth, seated 4,000 people and cost $3,000. It weighed 1,200 pounds with guy ropes and lines weighing 770 pounds. Its six sections were sewn together like a circus tent. The outer edge of the canvas came to an end nine feet from the ground.

The three main center poles were fifty-four feet long and a foot and one-half in diameter. The center pole was topped by a white flag with the red Christian cross. It is believed that part of one pole remains in the cupola of the Tabernacle today, having served as the flagpole on the Tabernacle that preceded the cross. It now forms one side of the ladder that leads to the hatch in the cupola from which the lights for the cross can be serviced.

This view of worshipers under the tent was probably taken from the preachers' stand. Note the oil lamps on posts and the people in their heavy clothing — in August.

The preachers' stand and benches under the canvas tabernacle erected in 1869. The forest of trees had given way to a forest of poles, and the canopy of leaves replaced by a canopy of canvas.

The Vineyard Grove Company Highland wharf looking toward East Chop, which was adopted by the MVCMA as its official landing. People and heavy carts and wagons loaded with baggage could now avoid the long trek over tedious hills and down the sandy roads that had once been the only way to the campgrounds.

The Other Side of the Fence

1870~1878

"The campground proper is filling up to repletion, and must, we think, should no accident befall it, always remain the nucleus of this great summer resort."

REV. HEBRON VINCENT, 1869

As the last quarter of the nineteenth century neared, three distinct communities, together making up approximately three hundred acres, now occupied the area where only the small grove of venerable oaks, Butler's sheep pasture, and scrub bushes had once existed.

Although all had their genesis in 1835, when the small group of Island believers first met to hold camp-meeting, each was unique in character and purpose. The MVCMA was made up of small cottages and tents and was still devoted to its religious purposes. It tried hard to protect that, even building a seven-foot picket fence in 1869 at a cost of just over $1,150. The fence was described as a "high green painted board fence constructed so very high as to prevent anyone from looking over the top unless a ladder was employed." The gateways, where people passed freely in and out during the day, were locked at 10 p.m. and reopened at the first streaks of daylight, about 5:30 a.m.

Although some have said the fence was erected to keep the influences of "sin city" at bay, it was actually constructed to protect and maintain the boundaries of the Association and to help keep order when the campgrounders were saying their prayers and preparing for bed. There were tales of the loose picket or two where people could crawl through if they were running late in returning back to their cottages or tents.

On the other side of the fence, the OBC, which had arrived in 1866, had set about establishing a busy resort town. And the Vineyard Grove Company (VGC), formed in 1869 by campground members, was designed to provide an overflow of land if and when the Camp-Meeting Association needed it.

The OBC was the most aggressive. It invested in the key elements of transportation and communication, the infrastructure necessary for development. Besides building the wharf that made it easier for visitors to arrive from the mainland, it invested $20,000 in the Old Colony Railroad extension from Monument Beach to Woods Hole to complete the service from Boston. The OBC also signed a contract in 1875 with the Western Union Telegraph Company to lay underwater telegraph cable from Falmouth to its resort.

Great strides were being made to develop a festive resort, and new structures appeared almost

As recreation grew in importance, Lake Anthony provided a quiet and safe sailing venue.

overnight, including some distinctive buildings that would survive into the twenty-first century. Most familiar is Union Chapel, a nonsectarian house of worship with an octagonal shape and stained glass windows, erected in 1870; and the OBC's crowning glory, the 175-room Sea View Hotel, built in 1872 and destroyed by fire in 1892.

Realizing the importance of keeping good relations with the Camp-Meeting Association, the OBC built the Arcade Building, still in existence on Circuit Avenue, to serve as offices and as a liaison between the Company and the MVCMA. The OBC also put up an octagonal pavilion pagoda where refreshments were sold, a tower where people could view the sights, and a six-hundred-foot plank walk from the wharf along the shore where people could promenade. It purchased additional real estate, paved streets, and laid out parks.

Lots in the resort were for sale, and construction of individual residences was well under way. Although the new housing was on a larger scale, the influence of the tiny campground cottages had reached the new resort. Many of the homes included the centered double doors on the front-facing gable end flanked by lancet windows on the ground floor, the second-floor set of double doors leading out to a balcony cantilevered over the entrance. The forty-five-degree pitch of the roof was decorated with gay, and sometimes flamboyant, gingerbread filigree trim.

The bustling resort, blossoming in just over thirty years from such a desolate spot, impressed a visiting reporter from the *New York Times*.

He mentions the immense crowds and the many cottages, hotels, and eating establishments. He told of the nightly hops, the bands, the sailing races, a beautiful landlocked harbor for sportsmen, and a trotting park.

The Vineyard Grove Company Highland wharf as seen from where the East Chop Beach Club is today. The freight office is visible to the right. A steamer and a two-masted sailing craft are both in the photo.

A view of Clinton Avenue; families had by this time begun to spend more and more of their summers at their homes on the campground.

When President Grant came to town

President Grant and members of his party on the porch of Bishop Haven's cottage, where Grant and his wife (far right) stayed during their visit to the Vineyard.

THE BIG EVENT of 1874 was the visit of President Ulysses S. Grant, the first U.S. president to visit the Vineyard. He came at the invitation of Rev. O. F. Tiffany, the minister of Grant's church in Washington, D.C., and was a guest of the MVCMA.

The president arrived at the Vineyard Highland Wharf on the *River Queen* with his wife and various state and national dignitaries. A gaily decorated horse-drawn trolley was waiting to take him and his party to Bishop Haven's Cottage (10 Clinton Avenue), where he and his wife would be staying. People lined the streets waving banners and shouting words of welcome, while an enthusiastic crowd waited to greet him at the cottage.

The whole town was decorated with lanterns, banners, flags, and streamers. Brass bands marched through the town playing patriotic music. President Grant and his party viewed a fireworks show, held in his honor, from the balcony of Harrison H. Tucker's home on Ocean Park. Grant's itinerary included services in the canvas tabernacle. He also visited Nantucket and Cape Cod.

This early interior view of Trinity Methodist Church was taken before the pews were added by the congregation. The flexible seating allowed for a variety of uses.

He was impressed with the layout of the town with its plank walks, bathing houses, and five miles of bathing beaches.

The reporter also pointed out the distinct division of the secular and religious communities and the order that prevailed throughout the area. "There are no dram-shops, no rowdies, no disturbances. Thieves do not break through nor steal. Rooms can be left open and trunks unlocked. The utmost order and quiet prevail everywhere."

Having strong ties to the campgrounds, the atmosphere was decidedly different on the northwest side of the camp-meeting grounds, where the VGC owned undeveloped land. Faced with the Association's refusal to buy the land from them, owners of the property, originally members of the camp-meeting association, sold additional shares to other Methodists. The new company acquired more holdings including the beach and waterfront in what is now Oak Bluffs, and hired a surveyor to plot lots, parks, and avenues. The surveyor was instructed to reserve a large area for holding religious services in the hopes that the Association would change its mind and decide to expand there. By the end of the first year the landowners had sold over $12,000 worth of lots, all adhering to the rules and regulations of the MVCMA.

The VGC built the Highland Wharf in 1872, which the MVCMA adopted as its official landing, and a plank walk extending from the wharf to the Association grounds. Now, people and carts and wagons, heavy with baggage, did not have to travel over tedious hills and down the sandy roads. A horse-drawn trolley providing transport to and from the campgrounds would be added later, making the

A view of the newly built (1878) Trinity Methodist Church probably taken from the roof of the preachers' stand. Note the perimeter frame and a couple of guy wires for the main posts of the canvas tent.

trip an even easier one.

In addition, the VGC built the sixty-room Highland House at the corner of East Chop Drive and Highland Drive. It built a bridge across Squash Meadow Pond, dividing it into what is now Sunset Lake and Lake Anthony, and a 3,500-foot plank walk that skirted the pond. Reluctant as the owners of the VGC had been to enter into the development business, they had done so with great speed.

Although the MVCMA was now flanked by two expanding communities, there was little room or demand on the campgrounds itself for more growth. Many of the tents had been replaced by cottages — 250 by 1869, 500 by 1880. The cottages were clustered on narrow avenues and pathways in the circles and parks, each with a pretty little veranda decorated with flowers and shells and a small garden in front. Window frames were decorated with scroll work, stained glass, silver doorplates, and hanging lanterns. Many of the houses were gaily painted and with furnishings ranging from simple to elegant with carpets, lace curtains, sofas, easy chairs, pictures, books, vases filled with flowers, and even an occasional piano.

The era of the large church/society tents was ending. Those with families and those now residing in the grove for longer periods of time preferred the privacy of smaller family tents or newly constructed cottages. The last of the society tents was removed in July 1882. After forty-seven years they had come, as one campgrounder remarked, to seem "almost like living friends."

Life in many ways was becoming easier. Additional bakeries, fresh food markets, and provision stores "well-furnished with all the luxuries of the season" were added. Many women or servants cooked over open fires to supplement food brought

An interior view of the Hammond Mill owned by John S. Hammond. Many of the designs shown can be seen on cottages on and off the campgrounds.

from home, and there were several cookhouses and a beanery where meals were served.

The feeling of confidence and excitement following the Civil War continued into the 1870s. Money was plentiful, and people were looking for speculative investments. Many found the Vineyard a perfect place. While they purchased and developed land around what is now Oak Bluffs, they also went into Edgartown and Katama.

Some of the off-island camp-meeting attendees, who had formed a strong attachment to Wesleyan Grove, chose to make the Vineyard their year-round home. Among them were the Frank Vincents, whose son, Wesley Grove Vincent, was born in the winter of 1871 and was the first child born on the campgrounds. Year-round residents of the campgrounds began holding church fellowship meetings at the residence of Capt. Joseph Dias, owner of the Vineyard Grove House. On June 3, 1877, the group was formally recognized as the Trinity Methodist Congregation, and the MVCMA erected a church the next year on the spot where several society tents had been located within Trinity Park. The new church seated approximately 250 and cost $7,748.

The Association built Grace Chapel in 1885 at the request of the women leaders of the Methodist church to house their many and varied activities.

An exterior view of one of the four mills mentioned that produced building materials and decorative trim —
the Hammond Mill, the Fisher and Huxford planing mill built in 1871 next to the Highland Wharf, the
Cottage City Novelty Works built in 1880, and the Bellview Heights planing mill.

The Howland family tent at 11 and 19 County Park (now Wesleyan Grove) with the Swiss Cottage to the right. The Swiss Cottage was prefabricated in New Bedford and erected at 8 County Park in 1868. The entire front of the cottage opened with a series of folding doors.

The Perez Mason Tower Cottage, designed by the campgrounds' chief architect, has long since disappeared.

A group of people, including Rev. L. B. Bates (in center), in front of the chapel tent on the Vineyard Highlands. Bates preached for many years at camp-meetings and was one of the men responsible for purchasing the land to form the Highlands.

These included the Ladies Missionary Society, which had been active since it held its first official meeting on the campgrounds in 1861. The Chapel, built on the west side of Trinity Park for $2,000, was later moved to 40 Trinity Park, the site of the Bethel Tent erected in 1860 by Rev. James D. Butler from New Bedford for his seamen parishioners. The chapel is now the United Methodist Church Parish House.

Rev. L. B. Bates prepares to address the crowds from the preachers' stand.

Despite these positive signs, however, a series of economic setbacks on the mainland, climaxing with the post–Civil War overexpansion of the railroads, resulted in economic uncertainty and a loss of confidence. The depression that followed lasted until the early 1880s, and the development boom on the Vineyard that started in 1866 came to an end. Property values fell, and real estate languished. Both the OBC and the VGC had overexpanded, were in debt, and faced problems from which they would never fully recover.

The OBC was particularly hard hit. During its sixteen years in business, it spent about $300,000 in the development of the resort and never paid a dividend to the six partners. The partners began selling some of the assets to cover their debts, including the beautiful Sea View Hotel. The remaining lots were sold at auction in 1882.

With no hopes that the Association would expand or move to the lands set aside for it, the VGC recouped some of its losses by inviting the Baptist congregation to locate a camp-meeting site on land already designed for the purpose.

Baptists had attended the camp-meetings in Wesleyan Grove for years, as one of many of the other denominations welcomed by the Methodists. Their numbers had increased to a point that they formed their own organization in 1875 and held a camp-meeting the week prior to the Methodist gathering. The Baptist camp-meetings proved so successful that in the fall of 1877 they authorized the construction of a wooden temple. It was built in 1878 at a cost of $3,187. The temple was used well into the 1920s, but as interest waned, the Baptists relocated their meeting to the north of Boston, and the structure gradually fell into disrepair. It was sold in 1937 to the Highland Property Trust, and in 1939 was finally torn down.

The original stockholders in the VGC were replaced by businesspeople with no connection to the MVCMA. The company went through a series of managements and was sold in 1920 to a mainland-based group.

By the late 1800s, only the MVCMA was thriving, primarily because it stayed true to its original purpose and never ventured into land speculation or other commerce.

Memories of a visitor

THROUGH THE YEARS, visitors have recorded their comings and goings to the camp-meeting. In 1869, one unnamed visitor painted an unflattering picture of what he found:

✳ He tells of the difficulty in traveling to the camp-meeting. First the "tempest passage with no shelter from the flying spray," on a sloop from Falmouth followed by the arduous walk on a narrow plank walk over the fine soft sand, most arriving at the site hot, thirsty, and generally uncomfortable. Lucky was the person who was able to purchase passage by wagon for ten cents.

✳ Upon arrival he was met and questioned by the campground guardian. If visitors did not have accommodations, they were assigned to a community tent half filled with straw with instructions to pick a corner and bed down when the time came.

✳ The eating house was a canvas-covered framework under which were arranged long tables and benches. The main dish, served three times a day, was an unnamed chowder prepared in large caldrons and served by a "perspiring" man with a pail attached to an end of a pole.

✳ There was a lengthy "code of regulations" which pertained to "almost everything connected with human life" and policed by duly appointed guardians of law, order, and morals.

✳ That evening lanterns were lit around the area. The community tent where he was to stay had a single lantern hanging from a pole inside and one at the entrance. After he entered the tent and carefully stepped over the "prone bodies of sleepers," he found a space and burrowed into the straw. Suddenly, a "sour-faced old maid" sat up and shrieked, 'Don't you dare to get your dirty boots on my clean stockings, you nasty man."

✳ Awaking the next morning, he sought a place to clean up. "An attendant beside a pump nearby informed me that I could wash my face there for fifteen cents. 'Towel and soap'll cost you five cents more and if you want a comb for your hair, that'll be five cents too!' he offered. I availed myself of these facilities wondering how many persons had used that comb and hoping that all were healthy."

The Fourth Street Avenue plank walk helped protect walkers moving toward Commonwealth Square.
Note the barber pole on the left.

Designed by J. W. Hoyt, the famous iron Tabernacle, located at the heart of the MVCMA grounds, was built in 1879 for a cost of $7,147.84. This view is taken from Trinity Methodist Church with the main entrance of the Tabernacle on the left.

A Place of Nobility and Beauty
1879

"It's an architectural gem, an historic treasure, a gathering place like no other, and only to be found on the Vineyard. Praises be!"

DAVID MCCULLOUGH, AUTHOR AND HISTORIAN

The Camp-Meeting Association had watched with interest the construction of the wooden temple built to serve the Baptist camp-meeting. Its own ten-year-old canvas tabernacle, first used in 1869, was showing wear. Association members realized they needed a more permanent structure that did not contain the heat or collapse during heavy windstorms. Now, the Association decided to solicit bids for its own wooden building.

Competing designs for wooden structures came from three architects with S. S. Woodcock, a well-known Boston architectural firm, submitting the winning design. The Association had budgeted $7,200, but the seventeen construction bids opened in March 1879 ranged from $10,000 to $15,000. The costs were both disappointing and surprising, since it cost just over $3,000 to build the wooden Baptist Temple a year earlier.

Unwilling to give up but looking for an alternative, the Association welcomed an idea from J. W. Hoyt, a campgrounder connected with an engineering and iron building firm in Springfield, Massachusetts. He told the Association he thought he could build an iron tabernacle for $6,200. A contract was signed on April 25 with his firm, Dwight and Hoyt, and the iron tabernacle was completed just ninety-two days later.

It was something of an engineering and transportation feat. The iron supports were shipped from Phoenixville, Pennsylvania, and Springfield — some by rail to Woods Hole, then steamer to the Highland Wharf, and horse-drawn railroad to the campgrounds. The largest sections were conveyed by boat down the Connecticut River and up Long Island Sound to Vineyard Sound.

Hoyt arrived the third week of May to supervise construction. The ground was cleared and prepared for the structure.

The four crosses

Dagnall collection

This cross was the third one to top the Tabernacle and was there for forty years.

A FLAGSTAFF FLYING a white flag with a red Christian cross topped the Tabernacle until 1926. The flagstaff was replaced with the first electric cross inspired by John Goss, the first layman to become president of the Association. It was destroyed in the hurricane of 1944.

A committee raised $1,376 to replace the cross. This cross, erected in 1950, was made of polished stainless steel and weighed about 350 pounds. It was eleven and a half feet high, and the arms were just over seven feet wide. It had sixty-six electric bulbs.

The cross was destroyed during a winter storm in the late 1960s. A third cross, designed by Gordon MacGillvray, longtime Association vice president and chairman of the Building and Grounds Committee, was placed on the Tabernacle in 1969 and served for nearly forty years.

The current cross was erected in 2008. The new carbon fiber cross is twenty feet tall and is topped by a two-foot lightning rod. The design of the cross is a compromise between the original tall and slender flagstaff and the crosses it replaced. It weighs approximately 180 pounds, with the cross itself weighing about eighty-five pounds. It is fastened to the Tabernacle with four stainless-steel bolts into a collar around what is believed to be one of the original center poles of the canvas tent that later served as the flagstaff.

A very early view of the Tabernacle interior. The wooden benches extended all the way to the front of the stage, and there was an earthen floor.

This view of the Tabernacle shows the main entry prior to the construction of the front entrance tower in 1901. Note the corrugated iron arch.

The benches were set aside and would be placed within the new Tabernacle when the structure was completed. Iron sections and skilled workers from Springfield, there to assemble the iron sections began to arrive June 9. The *Vineyard Gazette* reported on June 13 that the first section had been raised. Construction proceeded rapidly: the four main trusses were in place on June 24, and by July 1 the building was more than half completed. On July 19 it was reported that, "The frame is all up — light and graceful — the dome is complete and two sections of the corrugated-iron roofing have been put on." A mid-July completion date was promised.

The only delays were a strike at the rolling mills and an accident, happily not a serious one, at the site. And the final cost was $7,147.84 — just under the Association's budget.

The first service in the new Tabernacle was held on July 26, 1879. On the occasion of the dedication service eleven days later, a reporter from the *Cottage City Star* described the structure as an "object of nobility and beauty" and said that it had the approval of the surrounding community "on account of its first class accommodations."

Ellen Weiss, a noted architectural historian and author of *City in the Woods*, describes the Tabernacle as "an extraordinary nineteenth-century building, a product of the remarkable development in architectural engineering that allowed architects to create buildings with soaring lightness and beauty heretofore unknown and scarcely imagined."

The Tabernacle appears to be oval in shape, but the base is actually centered around a square formed by four main trusses from the Phoenix Iron Works placed forty feet apart and continuing upward to form a square upper roof. These trusses arch toward each other and meet at the center about seventy-five feet above the floor. They are rigidly joined together by four horizontal trusses and are the only perimeter pieces joined metal-to-metal.

The smaller iron pieces from Springfield, Massachusetts, are wood-jointed, giving the structure the flexibility to withstand high winds. This feature also made construction on uneven ground easier by not having to retool the metal on site. The original dirt floor, covered with sand to cut down dust, was replaced with a wooden floor and later, in sections, with concrete.

Three tiers of great hovering roofs, plus the cupola, float above a nearly circular space that is about 130 feet in diameter and supported only by a minimal web of angle irons. The roofs, which were originally corrugated iron, were replaced in 1931 with a corrugated concrete asbestos material. The roofs are separated from each other by two bands of clerestory windows.

There are forty-eight windows in each clerestory, the lower windows set horizontally and the upper windows set vertically. All of the windows consist of two clear center panes surrounded by yellow/brown panes on the sides and ends with either blue or red panes in the corners. While the top roof is square in shape, the two lower roofs have progressively rounded corners, so that the building appears nearly circular at the base.

Hoyt's influence in the design of the Tabernacle is obvious in the two cottages he designed (39 Butler Avenue and 18 Trinity Park), in which you can see the square shape of one and the square tower with stained glass windows of the other.

The Tabernacle is the largest covered venue on the Vineyard, seating between 2,000 and 2,500.

Croquet being played in the main circle. The game of croquet became a popular pastime in the 1860s for young and old alike. It became a problem when the clergy arrived late for services and was banned from the main circle in 1868.

The Stanton Sanders Cottage at 78 Trinity Park has flanking windows on the second floor and cutaway corners on the first. The elaborate trim rising from the window sills, visible in this photo, inspired the label of "Flame Cottage."

At one time, the benches, designed in 1861 and used in the canvas-topped building and reused in the new iron Tabernacle, extended all the way to the stage. Later, some of the benches fell into disrepair and were replaced by chairs. A receipt found in Association records documents a purchase of chairs in 1894 for sixty cents each.

The Tabernacle has undergone extensive repairs and care beginning less than ten years after its construction. Two major restoration projects have been undertaken in its 131-year history. In 1901, with the building rapidly deteriorating, the entire back extension was removed and rebuilt, and the structure was jacked up to renew the masonry supports. A tower was added to the front entrance. It is thought that the palladium windows over the stage were added at this time.

This was the last time any major structural design changes were made. The total cost for the restoration project was $5,500, and Association board minutes describe 1901 as "the year in which the Tabernacle was rebuilt."

Just over a century later, the Tabernacle underwent a second restoration project which included stabilizing the building, painting the iron-work, restoring the cupola, replacing the cross, and rebuilding the clerestory walls and windows. The total cost to date is almost $3 million.

The Tabernacle, declared a federal "Save America's Treasures" project in 2000, stands at the heart

MVCMA collection

View looking toward the Association Building and past early cottages on Trinity Park.

of the MVCMA grounds sheltering the original consecrated preaching area of 1835. It is the hub of religious and cultural activities on the Vineyard. During the summer season there is a full schedule of religious activities that includes regular Sunday services, Bible study groups, and Junior Camp-Meeting. There are evening concerts and performances on the weekends and Community Sings on Wednesday nights.

With its marvelous acoustics and beautiful setting, musical groups, individual performers, theater groups, choruses, and the Boston Pops Esplanade Orchestra find enthusiastic audiences in the Tabernacle. It is used for special Vineyard functions such as the Martha's Vineyard Regional High School and Oak Bluffs School graduations, and the All Island and Junior Art Shows.

The wooden tabernacle erected by the Baptists, which had inspired the construction of the Association's tabernacle, has long since been destroyed by time. Yet the MVCMA's iron Tabernacle continues to stand today as a beacon for sailors and Vineyarders.

People often come to the Tabernacle to show friends the unique structure, or to enjoy a moment of peace. Television personality Diane Sawyer says, "The Tabernacle draws me in every season. I love to bring guests, stand them in the center, force them to sing a round or hymn, and hear them sigh with pleasure. Such acoustics, such history, such comfort."

A view of Fourth Street Avenue, named for the Fourth Street Methodist Church of New Bedford, Massachusetts. Note the plank roadway that led from the Wesley House to the Tabernacle.

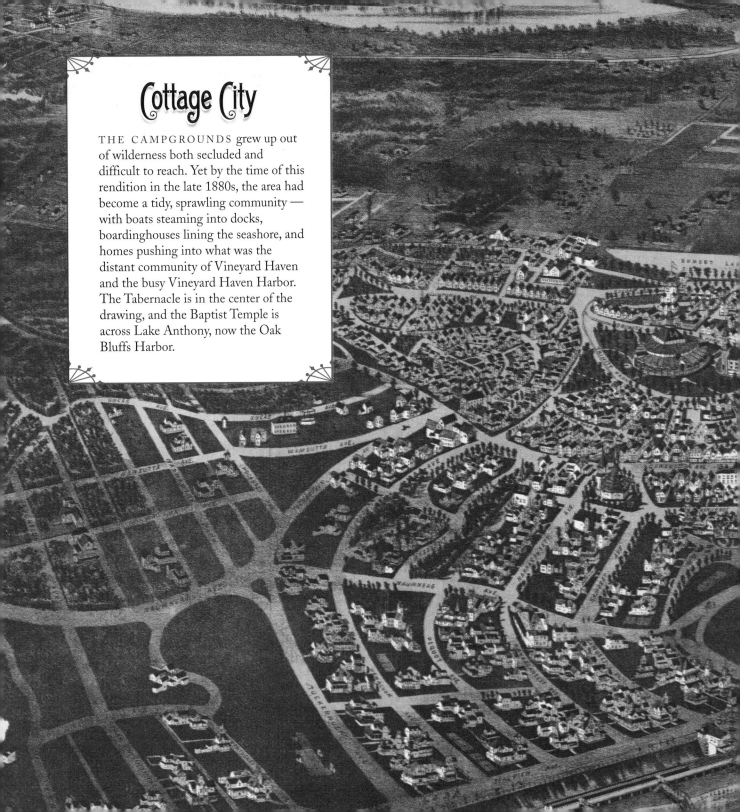

Cottage City

THE CAMPGROUNDS grew up out of wilderness both secluded and difficult to reach. Yet by the time of this rendition in the late 1880s, the area had become a tidy, sprawling community — with boats steaming into docks, boardinghouses lining the seashore, and homes pushing into what was the distant community of Vineyard Haven and the busy Vineyard Haven Harbor. The Tabernacle is in the center of the drawing, and the Baptist Temple is across Lake Anthony, now the Oak Bluffs Harbor.

A view of 2 Cottage Park built in 1869. This cottage has cutaway corners on the first floor. Note the welcoming sign atop the second-floor balcony.

Breaking Down the Barriers
1880~1909

"There is more real comfort and real enjoyment, both religious and secular, here than at any watering place I have ever visited."

COTTAGE CITY STAR

The year-round residents of the campgrounds and surrounding areas had, by 1870, begun to see a common enemy: Edgartown, the whaling village a few miles away that still had legal claim to all the land on which they lived. Edgartown collected their taxes and handed down orders on how they could live, but seemed to have little interest or consideration for the needs of the people living in this new and growing area.

The few people who lived mostly in Eastville, just outside Vineyard Haven (and near where the current hospital is), began thinking about secession in 1825. A petition was gathered in 1836 asking to be separated from Edgartown, but having little political power, the effort was dropped. But as the years passed and more people moved into the area, the idea of governing themselves became more and more attractive to those in the campground, the OBC resort, and Eastville.

In many ways, Edgartown had brought the problem on itself. Residents of the new communities became incensed when they saw their tax dollars being used to build Beach Road and the Martha's Vineyard Railroad from Oak Bluffs to Katama via Edgartown, in an effort to siphon off tourists from the growing resort.

By the time the grumbling had grown into a chorus, the state took action and agreed to make the area its own town. On February 17, 1880, the governor signed the bill dividing the old town of Edgartown, thus forming a new town which extended beyond the campgrounds and the resort town and included the areas of Eastville, Farm Neck, Lagoon Heights, and the Highlands.

The question of naming the new town posed a problem. The Post Office had used the names Vineyard Grove and Oak Bluffs at different times. The residents of the Highlands and the campgrounds favored naming it Vineyard Grove, and the residents of the resort town were in favor of Oak Bluffs. Neither side would budge. The name Cottage City was a compromise proposed by H. A. Blood, a former mayor of Fitchburg, Massachusetts, and a summer resident of the resort town. (The name Cottage City lasted until 1907, when the town's name was officially changed to Oak Bluffs.)

Cottage City was now a most desirable place for vacationers. It had balmy sea breezes, a spectacular view of Vineyard Sound, and long stretches of beaches perfect for sea bathing. The resort town was well laid out with beautiful parks and a thriving commercial center. At the time of its secession, Cottage City's valuation was estimated at $1,197,435 with fifteen hotels among its 1,058 taxable buildings. Its valuation ranked it 142nd in taxable value among the 306 Massachusetts towns. The first United States Census taken in 1880 showed the population of the new town to be 672.

Yet the era of rapid growth had ended. More people were living there year-round, and tourism had become the primary source of income. Although the campgrounds and the rest of Cottage City had two very different purposes, each shared areas of concern that made their cooperation imperative: sanitary facilities, water supply, and fire protection.

Because of the large number of people and the limited supply of fresh water, lack of adequate and proper sanitary facilities was a constant concern. Each season there were sporadic cases of dysentery or typhoid, but the fear was that unfavorable weather might produce conditions that could trigger an epidemic.

Children — including the well-cared-for lad in the carriage — play near the public water pump in Domestic Square (now Commonwealth Square) in 1870.

The Cottage City Water Company was established in the early 1880s. By the end of 1884, the privately owned company had installed 1,800 feet of cast-iron pipe from Squash Meadow Pond through the campgrounds to Circuit Avenue to provide sufficient water to fight fires. A few years later, when the water company completed a pumping station on the small fresh water pond at the head of the Lagoon, residents of town were supplied with safe drinking water. Because the State Board of Health issued an order directing the use of water from the wells on the campground be abandoned, residents were forced to connect to the water company. Despite strict rules about disposal of wastes, including cleaning of privies, it wasn't until 1903 that flush toilets arrived.

An interior view of the Spinney Cottage, made up of two cottages joined by a tower, located at one time at 2 Clinton Avenue. Many of the cottages by this time were owned by wealthy families who decorated their summer homes with elaborate furnishings and wall decorations.

The Crystal Palace is on the left in this photo, and the present-day MVCMA Cottage Museum is on the right. The lush plantings helped create beautiful roads and pathways.

This view of "Wee Hoos" hints at the hand of Perez Mason, designer of the Association Building, with its distinctive ornamental treatments.

A peaceful view of a simple Martha's Vineyard Campground Cottage with children enjoying the shade of the trees. Note the continuous arch over windows and door found on many campground cottages.

Cesspools began to replace the privies that were finally condemned in 1911.

A request was made at a town meeting in 1884 for additional water, fire service, and equipment. By the end of the year, there were two hydrants on the campgrounds and five more on Circuit Avenue. Additional water pipes were laid through the campgrounds in 1890, and by 1892, there had also been an increase in fire protection efforts. By then, there were seventy-seven volunteer firemen and one paid engineer who slept in the engine house that housed a steam fire engine, two eighty-gallon chemical engines, a hook and ladder truck, an independent hose wagon, and two independent hose carts. By then, according to a Sanborn map of Cottage City in 1892 showing the water distribution system of the town, the fire house was protecting a summer population of 15,000 to 20,000 and the winter population of 800, with 1,500 cottages and nine hotels.

The possibility of fire had always been a concern. As early as 1835 each tent was required to keep a bucket of water at the front or rear entrance. A disastrous Vineyard Haven fire in 1883, when most of the village center was destroyed, renewed the demand for an adequate supply of water and fire-fighting equipment.

Concern about fires was dramatically proven correct during the early to mid-1890s, which saw a rash of major fires, starting with the Sea View House and the skating rink, followed by the Highland House a year later. Fire protection in all three blazes was ineffective, and all the buildings were destroyed. There followed a series of fires putting everyone in the town on a "fire-bug" alert. Efforts were made to increase the much-needed water supply and firefighting equipment.

The concern about fires became a reality for campgrounders when a fire was discovered inside the Wesley House in November 1894. Although the damage was extensive, the fire did not break through the walls, thanks to the early discovery by two men who raised the alarm. Three days later, Gus Wesley, owner of the Wesley House, was arrested for arson. As with the Wesley House, the previous hotel fires had occurred at night in deserted buildings, leading to the suspicion that the fires had some connection with the troubled financial climate.

While the residents of Cottage City worked together under the new town government to form a cohesive community, it was still important for each area to maintain its identity — the religious campgrounds, the residential Highlands, and the resort area with its commercial center along bustling Circuit Avenue.

The fence encircling the campgrounds, erected in 1869, was dilapidated and had to be replaced in 1886. In an effort to reach out to the town and to avoid the feeling of exclusiveness, while at the same time clarifying the boundary lines, the new fence was erected at half the original height of seven feet.

The Association had always welcomed everyone who wished to participate in its religious programs, but to be more inclusive it began to include secular programs. While several meetings had been held in the Tabernacle on the secession issue, another, more charming and engaging way of reaching out emerged: the now famous Illumination Nights.

The Oak Bluffs Land and Wharf Company had sponsored the first gala illumination in 1869, probably as a promotional event advertising lots for sale in the new resort. In 1877 all the steamers serving the Island spent all day on Friday and early Saturday bringing people for Saturday night's Illumination. Thirty thousand men, women, and children were walking through the town and campgrounds enjoying the excitement and beauty of the evening. Because the massive crowds exceeded the limited accommodations, people doubled up in hotel rooms, tents, and cottages. The Sea View House set up beds in the dining room, steamers were utilized as hotels, and some even slept on the benches, under the canvas tent, and on the preachers' stand.

A few years later, sometime after the OBC ceased to exist and after Cottage City became a town in 1880, the Illuminations became centered on the MVCMA grounds. The year the Illuminations became part of the camp-meeting history isn't known. But certainly by Governor's Day, a new event established in 1903 and held in conjunction with the closing of the annual camp-meeting, Illumination night had become the climax of the camp-meeting.

Island-born Governor John L. Bates arrived at Cottage City as a guest of the Association on August 17, 1903. Bates, son of Rev. L. B. Bates, a Methodist evangelistic pastor who had preached at the camp-meetings on several occasions, was greeted at the steamship wharf by throngs of people. Along with local dignitaries and the officers of the Association, Bates paraded through the principal streets of Cottage City to the Wesley House.

After dining with the chief officers of the Asso-

Dagnall/Tucker collection

A view of the Bishop Haven Cottage. Years earlier, President Grant and his wife stayed here during their visit to the Vineyard in 1874.

ciation, the governor and his party attended services at the Tabernacle.

Governor's Day was very much a political affair, and Cottage City, with its vast crowds of visitors, was the perfect location. The day after his arrival, the governor made a whirlwind trip around the Vineyard meeting and greeting politicians in the major towns, ending up back at the Wesley House for dinner. That evening the governor, his party, and Association members marched two by two from the Wesley House down Fourth Street Avenue to attend the program at the Tabernacle. When the formal program was finished, the Tabernacle curtains were opened to reveal the circle of campground cottages decorated with hundreds of beautifully lighted lanterns.

Although the Governor's Days ended after almost thirty years, Grand Illumination has been magical for many generations. Eleanor McLeod Chase, born in 1900 and who had spent many summers on the campgrounds, remembered the "fairyland of lanterns and candles which were strung among the branches of the trees as well as along the eaves and porches of the houses."

At one time, the park area around the Tabernacle was decorated with more than 1,200 lanterns strung on wires criss-crossing the area. This practice was stopped in 1967 because of vandalism, theft, and the high cost of replacing the lanterns.

Illumination still centers around the Tabernacle.

Front-porch sitting — now much prized in the campgrounds — was a pleasant way of passing the days, as obvious in this photo of a cottage owned by a Dr. Tiffany on Clinton Avenue.

Although the campgrounds had grown literally from the wilderness, it is clear from this photo that a sophisticated society life had become the norm.

Grand Illumination is usually held on the third Wednesday evening in August. The Vineyard Haven Band begins the program, followed by a Community Sing after which the band continues to play while thousands parade throughout the campgrounds enjoying the many cottages decorated with colorful Oriental lanterns.

Each year a person or couple who have been actively involved in MVCMA activities is chosen as an honored guest to light the first lantern. This lantern is hung in the entrance to the Tabernacle as a signal to cottagers to light their lanterns, transforming the campgrounds into a magical fairyland.

In 1885, a great gathering assembled to celebrate the fiftieth anniversary of the first camp-meeting. Those attending included thirty-one men who had been present at the initial gathering on the same spot half a century earlier.

Rev. Hebron Vincent presented the principal address for the occasion. At eighty years of age, he was commanding in appearance, and his dark eyes sparkled as he recounted memories, especially when speaking of his brethren who "had long since gone to the other shore."

Vincent and the others had lived to see major changes in both the camp-meeting and the community around it. The camp-meeting services were more conventional now than revival, with no more "fervid whooping" in the woods. Cottages had replaced tents. The sheep pasture was now a village, and the land around it a town.

Yet bells continued to call the faithful to worship. Ezekiel, a bell located for years behind the Tabernacle, was given to the Swedish N.E. Church at Newport, Rhode Island, when a new Memorial Bell

W. Douglas Thompson collection

The house is ready for Illumination Night. It is now the MVCMA Cottage Museum.

was presented to the Association in 1888 by Sarah Cook in memory of her father, Hezekiah Anthony. The 1,500-pound memorial bell was placed in the tower of Methodist Trinity Church, where it remains today.

Although much had changed, much had also remained the same. A reporter from the *New York Times*, covering the 1885 event, wrote, "The Methodist camp-meetings are in full blast here."

View of the Wesley House from Lake Anthony (now Oak Bluffs Harbor), and showing what was then the rear entrance. The original Wesley House, built in 1878, later added adjacent buildings and a fourth floor to create the current hotel. It is one of the two original remaining boarding/lodging establishments.

Modern Days
1910~2010

"It is a wonderful thing to think of our glorious past and to contemplate a more glorious future."

BOARD MEMBER, EARLY 1900S

Martha's Vineyard — which had remained isolated and protected for centuries — was now firmly a part of the twentieth century. Five wars, a stock market crash followed by the Great Depression, advancements in technology and communication, and the age of the great industrialists and financiers: each would have its own impact on the Island and the campgrounds.

America was rapidly changing, and one of the trends was a loss of religious fervor. The intensity of the religious Third Great Awakening that began in the 1850s had diminished and was directed toward social activism in areas of education, child labor, women's rights, prohibition of alcohol, and a variety of missionary activities. It grew obvious in the 1930s and 1940s that the campgrounds, despite the dedication of Association members to retain both economic and religious strength, was especially vulnerable to the changes on the mainland.

The value of the cottages fell dramatically during the Depression years. Strapped by a poor economy and not feeling their cottages were especially valuable, some cottage owners stopped paying their lease fees and town taxes. (The Camp-Meeting Association has always held ownership of the land and leased it to cottage owners.) Cottages were sold for as little as $52.40 to cover back taxes and fees. In some cases, cottages, signed over to the Association by owners who could no longer keep them, were sold for less than what was owed for lease fees and taxes. This left the Association responsible for payment of any unpaid taxes to the town.

Other cottage owners deferred maintenance for almost two decades, causing some of the cottages to fall into disrepair and be torn down. One newcomer noted in 1952 that the famous gingerbread cottages looked forlorn and forsaken, with weather-beaten doors and shutters hanging loosely.

A view from Ellinwood Heights across bridge spanning Sunset Lake looking toward the campgrounds.

Attendance at the summer programs and camp-meeting week declined during these years, and collections fell about 30 percent. To compensate for the declining income, the Association deferred maintenance of its buildings and grounds and delayed purchasing equipment. Faced with choosing between a $65 horse and a $200 truck for transportation in 1935, the horse won.

Faced with the same decision six years later, when the economy had begun to improve, the truck won. According to a Board member at the time, this proved to be a profitable investment as the truck could do double the work and this "new horse" had to be fed only when it worked.

Some cottage owners, to help defray the expense of owning and maintaining their cottages, began in the mid-1930s to rent their campground homes through rental agencies. This brought about its own problems, since the Association started receiving complaints about renters who did not follow the rules that made living in such close proximity possible. Others had sold their cottages to people who did not support the religious mission of the camp-meeting, and therefore, along with many of the renters, did not attend the services. This added to the worries that the camp-meeting was straying far from its religious mission.

To handle the complaints and to try to increase attendance at the religious programs, the Association board in 1945 voted to take over all sales, transfers, and rentals of the cottages. This would ensure that those who purchased or rented cottages would respect the property, be sympathetic to the mission, and attend the religious services and programs. This rental practice lasted until the early 1960s, but the Association still must approve all cottage sales and lease transfers.

While the early founders of the camp-meetings in Wesleyan Grove were Methodist, the Association was never officially connected with the central organization of the Methodist Church, which had distanced itself from those early camp-meetings because of embarrassment over the evangelistic style of the services. As the popularity of the emotional, evangelical religious preaching faded, the format of the services changed to a more traditional ritual.

The MVCMA officially became interdenominational in 1931 as its leaseholders became a blend of many denominations.

Some were not happy with the changes, wanting the Association to remain as it had been founded. Camp-meeting records reflect the concern of a board member in the 1930s who reminded his fellow board members that the Association was founded for the express purpose of promoting the Protestant conception of the New Testament and, as late as 1955, the president at the time reminded the board that the Association was primarily a Methodist Association as was intended by the founding fathers.

Upon the celebration of the Wesleyan Grove Camp-meeting centennial in 1935, the *Vineyard Gazette* recognized the influence of the campgrounds on the Vineyard: "the camp-meeting dominated the Island's summer history for a great many years ... and brought the Island into flower as a vacation resort." A representative of the Association expressed hopes it would continue to contribute to the religious life of the community and the nation as it had in the past.

In an attempt to make this happen and to increase attendance at summer programs and during Camp-Meeting Week, the Association had for years

A view showing the Sea View House and Lake Anthony (still a freshwater pond) along what would later become Lake Avenue.

The Attleboro House was built in 1874 as a guest house (bottom). It was raised in 1890 (far left), along with a second cottage, to add a dining room, living room, and office, all on the first floor (above). The Attleboro continues to rent rooms during the season, but no longer serves meals.

The Association Building, designed by Providence architect Perez Mason, cost just under $1,000 to construct. It was located a short distance from the main circle near what was the main entrance to the grounds, now Clinton Avenue, and near the foot of what is now Trinity Park. The two-and-a-half-story building is twenty-four by forty-four feet and serves as the headquarters of the encampment.

been adding programs to appeal to residents of the Town as well as the campgrounders. The popular Community Sings, started in the early 1920s, became a regular part of the summer program along with a variety of secular programs.

Special services were held daily at the preachers' stand for children during the early 1840s. In the 1860s, one of the active ministers of the Association often met with the children to teach lessons. This could have been the inspiration for the Daily Vacation Bible School established in 1931, led by Mary D. Hatch, with over 100 children enrolled. The program was popular and attended by children of many denominations on the grounds and in the surrounding communities.

The continued success of the Bible School, now known as Junior Camp-Meeting, is the result of the efforts and dedication of the many teachers who provided, and continue to provide, a full program for children.

As the economic crisis began to ease, the campground programs slowly increased in attendance and returned to pre war brilliance.

With the end of the European war in May and the Pacific war in August, the Grand Illumination Night of 1945 was celebrated with hundreds of gaily lighted lanterns hung throughout the grounds surrounding the Tabernacle, and the Tisbury school orchestra provided the music.

The following year, much-needed maintenance on the Association buildings and cottages began. Gardens were planted with bright flowers. The paint brushes came out, and the cottages, like the gardens, bloomed with a wide variety of colors. Inflation began to creep into the campgrounds in 1943, and prices of the approximately four hundred cottages more than doubled by 1946.

Cottages that sold for $1,000 to $2,500 in 1950 were selling for $2,000 to $3,000 in the 1960s. The first cottage to sell for a five-digit number was in 1970, and by the end of the decade cottages were selling for five times that figure. Prices continue to rise to $150,000 in the 1980s and to $230,000 in the 1990s, reaching a peak of $650,000 in 2006.

Oak Bluffs and the MVCMA continue to change in the twenty-first century.

The MVCMA, 175 years old in 2010, remains a welcoming, strong, and unique organization combining many of the attributes of its past with the promise of the future.

The memories of fun summers on the Vineyard continue to be collected by each new generation. While life moves at a slower pace within the grounds, there is constant activity. Friends stop to chat with each other or hold neighborhood gatherings. People walk to nearby stores, work on their cottages or in their yards, or rock on their porches. Children ride bicycles, sell lemonade, or play games like hopscotch together.

Bible Study groups are held under the small tent erected in the summer near the Tabernacle, and twice a week the MVCMA has walking tours. There is choir practice on Saturday mornings, Sunday morning church services, and Camp-Meeting Week in July. Children parade on their bikes in the Fourth of July children's parade. There are the regular Wednesday night Community Sings, and the Tabernacle hosts dozens of programs during the week and on weekends, including concerts, movies, and lectures.

And, as in times past, residents return to their snug cottages in late evening, and all is quiet.

Sam Low collection

Sam Low collection

Moving a cottage

Sam Low collection

Cottages were easy to move with their lightweight construction and no plumbing or electrical connections. The cottage in these pictures was once located at 2 and 4 Rural Circle. It was moved in the early 1930s to its present location at 30 Martha's Park Road in Hart Haven. Note the traffic light (previous page) in the intersection of Circuit and Lake avenues, which has long since disappeared. Those involved in the move (above) help refurbish the cottage in its new location (right).

The walk-through Arcade Building, designed by S. F. Pratt, built by the Oak Bluffs Land and Wharf Company to serve as offices and as a liaison between the Company and the MVCMA.

"God bless you"

THE PAINTED COTTAGES of the campgrounds, wedged so tightly together, hold an endless fascination. There are stories of people sneezing and hearing a pleasant "God bless you" from someone three cottages away.

One story tells of a campgrounder returning from a very successful fishing trip and asking his wife, while in their kitchen, if she thought their next-door neighbor might like some fish. The wife, upon emerging from her front door on her way to ask the neighbor, found her neighbor coming out her front door holding a dish saying that she would very much like to have some of the freshly caught fish.

This photo shows Clinton Avenue, the only straight-line boulevard on the grounds and once the main entrance to the campgrounds.

Acknowledgments

THE INSPIRATION for this book comes from my own longtime connection to the campgrounds.

Both my family and my husband's family have connections with the campgrounds dating back to the early 1900s. My mother and her family stayed at one of the campground hotels, the Beatrice House, in the teens and twenties when my grandfather drove tours to Gay Head for the hotel. I began spending my summers here sixty-five years ago when my grandparents bought a campground cottage in 1946. My husband's great-grandparents owned the cottage at 8 Clinton Avenue during the same period and took in boarders. After renting on the campgrounds for ten years, his parents bought a cottage in 1958. Both families' cottages are now owned and enjoyed by us, our children, and their families.

We have a lifetime of memories. My husband and I met and were married here. We have lifelong friends and families living here. We have family members and friends who are buried here. The campground has become our home.

I BECAME INTERESTED in the history of the MVCMA in the summer of 1983 and discovered that, although there were references to the history of the MVCMA in a variety of publications, there was no one source for information.

The following summer I gathered what I could find, organized it, and completed my first book, *Martha's Vineyard Camp-Meeting Association 1835–1985*, in time for the Sesquicentennial of the MVCMA in 1985.

It was never my intention to write a second book, but in organizing information for writing the MVCMA National Historic Landmark application with Ellen Weiss in 2004, I realized how much information I had gathered over the years — enough for a second book. I also discovered I had made some errors in my first book, including stating that Hebron Vincent died in 1869. I am happy to report that he lived an additional twenty-one years.

After procrastinating for a couple of years, I began organizing the material I had gathered and started to write in 2009. I managed to complete a manuscript of over 70,000 words; the work had just begun.

This book would not have been possible without my very supportive husband Russ, who never complained when I disappeared into our office for hours at a time, was my first-, second-, and sometimes third-round proofreader, and encouraged me every step of the way. More assistance came from good friends Doug Ulwick, who proofread for historical accuracy, scanned picture after picture, drew illustrations, was a good sounding board, and was always there to provide help when needed; Ellen Weiss, my coauthor in writing the National Historic Landmark application and an invaluable source of architectural information; and Jan Pogue, my editor and publisher, who helped me transform my tome into a history with a story.

In addition, I would like to thank Eulalie Regan, former librarian at the *Vineyard Gazette*, who was as generous with her help as she was with sharing her mid-morning snacks; the MVCMA, whose records were made available to me; the many people who shared various bits of information with me; and those who provided the great pictures for this book from their personal collections.

Information continues to surface when least expected. I am sure there is more information out there — perhaps in someone's attic or basement or in little-known publications. Many times I wished I could go back in time loaded with a camera and tape recorder. But lacking that ability, I continue to gather the information that comes my way.
— SALLY DAGNALL

Mission Statement

THE MISSION of the Martha's Vineyard Camp-Meeting Association (MVCMA) is to hold Annual Religious Meetings on the Island of Martha's Vineyard as defined in our Act of Incorporation (May 1, 1868).

To support this mission we will:

* provide a wide variety of ecumenical religious programs such as Sunday Services, Campmeeting Week, Junior Camp Meeting, Hymn Sings, Bible Study, Philosophical Discussions, and Lectures to involve all of our Leaseholders and others interested in our mission.

* afford opportunities for activities such as the Flea Market, Craft Fair, Children's Festival, Pot Luck Suppers, etc. to create a feeling of community for our Leaseholders.

* present a wide variety of secular programs including Concerts, Lectures, Performances, Plays, Dances, Community Sings, etc. open to all Island residents and visitors.

* preserve the integrity, ambiance, and historical significance of our Community by maintaining our public buildings, roads, walkways and grounds.

* provide access to our archives and informational guidance to assist our Leaseholders in restoring and maintaining the historical appearance of our Community.

* maintain open communication with our Residential and Commercial Leaseholders by regularly reporting our actions and plans to provide avenues for their input by holding regularly scheduled Leaseholder Meetings, by being available to meet with small groups or individuals, and by providing a time at the beginning of each MVCMA Board Meeting for individuals to address the Board.

* further our relationship with the Island community by hosting School Graduations, Art Shows, Charitable Events, etc., and by providing scholarship aid for advanced education to graduates of the Martha's Vineyard Regional High School.

* share our heritage and historical significance of our Community and its status as a National Historic Landmark, commemorating the history of the United States of America, by welcoming visitors to our grounds.

Ratified at the MVCMA Board Meeting on May 28, 2005.

List of Firsts & Important Dates

1835

* One-half acre of land leased from William Butler Esq. The lease was arranged by Thomas M. Coffin, Jeremiah Pease, and Frederick Baylies.
* The encampment was referred to as the Vineyard Camp Meeting.
* First camp-meeting, August 24.
* First secretary of the camp-meeting, Hebron Vincent.
* First rules, read from the preachers' stand. Copies were posted and distributed in 1853. In 1858 a set of rules was formally adopted.

1836

* Land was leased on an annual basis from 1836 to 1839.
* First mention of the Love Feast.

1837

* First mention of boarding tents.

1838

* First camp-meeting held over the Sabbath.
* First mention of a trumpet calling people to the stand.
* First mention of the Sacrament.
* On April 17, an Act For Protection of Camp Meetings against disturbances was passed by the Massachusetts Legislature.

1840

* The first five-year lease was obtained on November 16, 1839, from Stephen H. and Harriet Bradley, who had purchased the land from William Butler plus additional adjacent lands. The lease was arranged by Thomas M. Coffin, Isaiah D. Pease, and Jeremiah Pease.
* The name Wesleyan Grove was formally adopted.
* First purchase of a book to keep official records of the meetings.
* First mention of small tents belonging to the larger society tents.
* First mention of the "usual" Parting Ceremony.

1841

* First mention of family tents.
* A Committee of Arrangements was appointed to maintain the grounds. This committee began to run the business side of the campgrounds in 1856.

1845

* The camp-meeting took place at Westport Point on the mainland.

1846

* A five-year lease (1846–1850) was obtained from Stephen H. and Harriet Bradley. The lease was arranged by Sirson P. Coffin, Charles Worth, and Charles Weeks.

* First mention of debt: $174.98.

1847

* The custom of holding preachers' meetings was adopted.

1848

* First mention of the need for early religious training for children.
* First mention that the Parting Ceremony had been replaced by a simple meeting and leave-taking in front of the preachers' stand.

1850

* An eleven-year lease (1850–1861) was obtained in the fall of 1849 from Stephen H. and Harriet Bradley. The lease was arranged by Sirson P. Coffin for $30 per year.
* Two additional parcels of adjacent land were obtained for $6.
* Total leased land was now somewhere between twelve to fifteen acres.
* The term Agent was formally adopted.

1851

* The Finance Committee was designated a Standing Committee.

1852

* A Committee on Order was appointed.

1853

* Copies of rules and regulations printed for distribution.

1854

* Vigilance Committee appointed.

* First time a policeman was hired to patrol the grounds.

1855

* First mention of family tents being required to be approved by the home church and having to post the name of the owner and the church on the tent.

1856

* First cottage, Rev. Upham's in the Cottage Park area.
* First mention of the erection of houses built of wood.
* First tax: a 50-cent tax was assessed for each tent. This was to cover the costs of maintaining the grounds. The community had to be watched, protected, lighted, and safeguarded in health.
* A treasury was established.
* First mention of a business meeting held off the campgrounds.

1857

* Jeremiah Pease died at 65 years of age.
* First mention of people arriving early.

1858

* With three years remaining on the last lease, a ten-year lease with rights to renew or to purchase at market value, was obtained from Stephen H. and Harriet Bradley (1858–1871). The lease was arranged by Sirson P. Coffin, Preston Bennet, and William Lawton of Providence, Abner L. Westgate of Fall River, and Henry Walker of New Bedford.

* First authorization was given to apply for a loan, not to exceed $1,000.

1859

* The Association Building was built for just under $1,000.
* First mention of bell placed near the preachers' stand.
* A 40-foot avenue encompassing the entire circle of tents — Asbury Avenue.

1860

* First formal organization formed (Articles of Agreement).
* The name, Martha's Vineyard Camp-Meeting Association, was fixed in the Articles of Agreement.
* First mention of a groundskeeper/agent — Sirson P. Coffin.
* First mention of commercial enterprises beginning to appear.
* First officers of the MVCMA:
  President: George M. Carpenter, presiding elder of the Providence District
  Secretary: Hebron Vincent of Edgartown
  Treasurer: Henry Bradley of Holmes Hole
  Agent: Sirson P. Coffin of Edgartown

1861

* All tents, houses, and cottages were required to be licensed and charged a fee to defray the expenses of preparation for the camp-meeting.
* A new preachers' stand and seating, designed by Perez Mason, were erected.
* First mention of tents/cottages being rented.

1863

* Street lamps installed.

1865

* The land previously leased was purchased for $1,300 from the Bradleys. Purchase included the rights of way. The sale was arranged by William B. Lawton, Abner L. Westgate, Caleb L. Ellis, and Kilborn Smith, who were authorized to take and hold the deeds of the same in trust for the Camp-Meeting Association. William B. Lawton, John Kendrick, and Charles H. Titus were appointed to raise the funds.
* The entire encampment was now twenty-six acres.
* First hotel of substance built (two-story wooden structure for boarding and lodging).
* First mention of State Police on the campgrounds.

1866

* Additional land was purchased, making a total of thirty-five acres.
* The Oak Bluffs Land and Wharf Company (OBC) was established.
* The wharf in Oak Bluffs built by the OBC.

1868

* The MVCMA was incorporated on May 1 by the Commonwealth of Massachusetts.

1869

* Additional land was purchased for $600, making total of thirty-eight acres.
* The first wedding on the campgrounds took

place (Adin B. Capron and Irene Ballou).

* The Vineyard Grove Company was formed.
* The mammoth canvas tent was put up.
* The first illumination, sponsored by the OBC, took place.
* The picket fence surrounding the campgrounds was built.
* The Women's Foreign Missionary Society of the Methodist Episcopal Church chapter met on the campgrounds on August 14.

1871

* The first child born on the campgrounds (Wesley Grove Vincent).
* The post office was established on the campgrounds.

1872

* The Arcade was built.

1873

* The horse-drawn railroad was completed.

1874

* President Grant visited the campgrounds.
* Baptists located their meetings on the Highlands.
* The Central House (Beatrice House) was built.
* The Attleboro House was built.

1878

* Trinity Methodist Church was built.

1879

* The Tabernacle was built.

* The Wesley House was built.

1880

* Cottage City was incorporated on February 17.

1885

* Grace Chapel was built.

1888

* The Memorial Bell was donated to the MVCMA by Sarah Cook for her father, Hezekiah Anthony.

1895

* The Electric Railway replaced the horse-drawn railway.

1900

* The official seal was adopted by the Association.

1901

* First major Tabernacle restoration project.

1903

* First Governor's Day was held on August 17.

1907

* Oak Bluffs was incorporated.

1910

* Presentation of Sunset Lake and surrounding area on October 28, 1910, to the Town of Oak Bluffs as part of its park system. Accepted by Town on May 25, 1911.

1919

✻ First mention of Community Sings.

Early 1920s

✻ The Community Sings became a regular part of the program.

✻ First Community Sing director Professor Warren P. Adams.

1923

✻ First layman elected president of the MVCMA — John Goss.

1926

✻ The first cross (electric) was placed on the Tabernacle.

1931

✻ First easement granted to the Town of Oak Bluffs for Lake Avenue and a sidewalk.

✻ The MVCMA officially became interdenominational.

✻ Daily Vacation Bible School began (Junior Camp-Meeting) — Mrs. Mary D. Hatch, leader.

1935

✻ The MVCMA Centennial.

1944

✻ First mention of a Leaseholders' Meeting.

1946

✻ First woman Board member mentioned in the records (Mary H. Hoyle).

1953

✻ Camp Jabberwocky started by Helen Lamb at 8 Commonwealth Avenue.

1957

✻ Second easement granted to the Town of Oak Bluffs on February 18 for bulkhead.

1961

✻ The Lantern Shop was started.

1967

✻ Last big Grand Illumination.

1973

✻ Campground fire, primarily involving cottages at 77, 78, and 79 Trinity Park.

1978

✻ The Commonwealth of Massachusetts nominated Wesleyan Grove to be listed on the National Register of Historic Places for being unique in the nation for its architecture, remarkable state of preservation, and as the best example of a nineteenth-century religious retreat.

1979

✻ The Tabernacle Centennial.

✻ MVCMA included in the National Register of Historic Places.

1982

✻ The Friends of Oak Bluffs presented an award to the MVCMA contributing to the beauty of Oak Bluffs.

1985

* The MVCMA Sesquicentennial.
* Presentation of a Sesquicentennial Proclamation by Governor Michael S. Dukakis of Massachusetts for being true to its founding principles and contributing to the enrichment of the commonwealth.
* First Museum at 33 Rock Avenue, later moved to 1 Trinity Park in 1990.

1988

* Land survey by Gordon MacGillvray.

1989

* First rubbish stickers sold for $1.00.

1990

* The area under Nancy's Snack Bar sold for $355,000.

1994

* First Campground Cottage Tour.
* The 911 System installed in Oak Bluffs.

1996

* MVCMA receives the Martha's Vineyard Preservation Trust Award for contributing to the preservation of historic Island structures.

1999

* First woman board president (Judith Foss).
* Tabernacle declared a "Save America's Treasures" project by First Lady Hillary Clinton.

2000

* Declared an official Save America's Treasures project.

2001

* Sewers installed.
* First $1,000 scholarship presented by the MVCMA to MV Regional High School graduate.

2002

* Second major Tabernacle restoration project.
* Presented the Bartholomew Gosnold Award by the Martha's Vineyard Preservation Trust and the Martha's Vineyard Historical Society for architectural preservation.

2004

* First Campground Walking Tour.

2005

* An unbuildable lot located at the site of the old New York Landing on Vineyard Haven Harbor sold for $275,000. The total acreage of MVCMA land is now 34.14 acres.
* Tabernacle declared a National Historic Landmark on April 5, 2005, by the Secretary of the Interior and the National Parks Service.
* Camp-Meeting Week revived.

2006

* New water mains installed by the Oak Bluffs Water District.

Bibliography

An Historical Walking Tour of Oak Bluffs. Oak Bluffs: Oak Bluffs Centennial Committee and the Oak Bluffs Historical Committee

Banks, Charles Edward, *History of Martha's Vineyard*. Boston: George H. Dean, 1911

Coe, June Melony, *A Guide To East Chop Families*. 1990

Dagnall, Sally W., *Martha's Vineyard Camp Meeting Association 1835–1985*. Oak Bluffs: The Association, 1984

Hough, Henry Beetle, *Martha's Vineyard Summer Resort After 100 Years*. Rutland, VT: Academy Books, 1966

Hough, Henry Beetle, *Summer Resort 1835–1935*. Rutland, VT: The Tuttle Publishing Co., 1936

Jones, Peter, *Images of America, Oak Bluffs, The Cottage City Years on Martha's Vineyard*. Chicago/Portsmouth/San Francisco: Arcadia Publishing, 2007

LeBaron, Ira. W., *The Campmeeting at Martha's Vineyard*. Nashville: Parthenon Press, 1958

Lobeck, A.K., *A Brief History of Martha's Vineyard Camp-Meeting Association*. Oak Bluffs, 1956

Mayhew, Eleanor R. (editor), *Martha's Vineyard, A Short History and Guide*. Edgartown: Dukes County Historical Society, Inc. 1956

Morrison, Rev. W.V., *Martha's Vineyard Campmeeting*. (Souvenir History) 1897

Norton, Henry Franklin, *Martha's Vineyard*. (History, Legends and Stories). The Pyne Printery, Hartford, CT, 1923

Railton, Arthur R., *The Story of Martha's Vineyard: How We Got to Where We Are*. In association with Martha's Vineyard Historical Society, Commonwealth Editions, Beverly, MA, 2006

Stoddard, Chris, *A Centennial History of Cottage City*. Oak Bluffs: Oak Bluffs Historical Commission, 1981

Vincent, Hebron, *A History of the Camp Meeting and Grounds at Wesleyan Grove, Martha's Vineyard for the Eleven Years Ending with the Meeting of 1869*. Boston: Lee and Shepard, 1870

Vincent, Hebron, *History of the Wesleyan Grove Camp Meeting From the First Meeting Held There in 1835 to That of 1858*. Boston: George C. Rand and Avery, 1858

Weiss, Ellen, *City in the Woods*. Boston: Northeast University Press, 1998

ONLINE

About Our Church, "Roots, 1736–1816," "The Churches Grow, 1817–1843," United Methodist Communications

"British Methodism and the Poor 1739–1999," Methodist Archives 7 Research Center

"Camp Meeting," Wikipedia, the free encyclopedia

"Camp Meetings," The Tennessee Encyclopedia of History and Culture

Cody, David, "The Victorian Web," The Methodist Church of Great Britain

"The United Methodist Church," Religious Movements Homepage: United Methodist Church

Wesley, John, "A Short History of Methodism," *The Works of John Wesley*, 1872

"What is a Campmeeting?" South Union Campmeeting

"A Brief History," Zion's Herald

Issues of the *Dukes County Intelligencer*:

"Setting the Stage for the Camp Meeting," Arthur R. Railton, Vol. 26, No. 4, May 1985, 139–154

Bits and Pieces, 184

"That First Camp Meeting," Vol. 26, No. 4, May 1985, 158–164

"The Wesleyan Grove Camp Ground — Some Old Photographs," Vol. 21, No. 1, August 1979

"How We Approved the Site," Hebron Vincent, Vol. 26, No. 4, May 1984, 155–157

"The Iron Tabernacle at Wesleyan Grove," Ellen Weiss, Vol. 21, No. 1, August 1979, 3–14

"The First Week in the Woods," Henry Baylies, Vol. 33, No. 3, February 1992

"Camp meeting of 1872 As Seen By Artists," Vol. 29, No. 2, November 1987

Vol. 8, No. 2, November 1966

Vol. 45, No. 1, August 2003

NEWSPAPERS

Cottage City Star

Vineyard Gazette, Edgartown MA

Tabernacle Centennial Issue, August 3, 1979

"1835 — Martha's Vineyard Camp Meeting — 1935", August 23, 1935

"Gingerbread Magic and Diversity: The Gracious Charm of Oak Bluffs Is Unity Woven of Many Threads," Della Brown Hardman, July 30, 1999

"Vineyard as Resort: Exploding the Myths," J.D. Kelley, July 30, 1999

"The Wesley House — A Reminder of Cottage City's 19th Century Summer Glory," Ruth Low, September 28, 1979

"Chase Family Era Comes to an End at Wesley House on the Oak Bluffs Harbor," Mark Alan Lovewell, August 16, 1985

"Wesley House Lore Was Rich Even on Diamond Anniversary," Henry Beetle Hough, August 16, 1985

Zion's Herald (newspaper of the Southern New England conference of the Methodist Church)

PERIODICALS

Wilson, Howard G., "Oh, To Be Young Again at Wesleyan Grove," *Yankee Magazine*, August 1959

Martha's Vineyard Camp Meeting Association (MVCMA) archives

MVCMA Application for National Historic Landmark

MVCMA Guided Walking Tours

Ness, John H., "Methodism," Encarta 98 Encyclopedia

Cyclopaedia of Methodism, Matthew Simpson, Philadelphia: Louis H. Everts, 1880

Butler, Clementina, "A Letter from Clementina," Response. Vol. 12, No. 4, The United Methodist Church, Cincinnati, Ohio, April 1980.

Index

"There is something peculiarly dear to me about the Vineyard.
There is not another place on earth
which ever seemed to me so much like paradise."

REV. FRANKLIN FISK
of Yarmouthport, Massachusetts, 1838